Math Achievement
Enriching Activities Based on NCTM Standards

Grade 8

by
Tracy Dankberg
and
Leland Graham

Table of Contents

Introduction

Welcome to the **Math Achievement** series! Each book in this series is designed to reinforce the math skills appropriate for each grade level and to encourage high-level thinking and problem-solving skills. Enhancing students' thinking and problem-solving abilities can help them succeed in all academic areas. In addition, experiencing success in math can increase a student's confidence and self-esteem, both in and out of the classroom.

Each **Math Achievement** book offers challenging questions **based on the standards specified by the National Council of Teachers of Mathematics (NCTM)**. All five content standards (number and operations, algebra, geometry, measurement, data analysis and probability) and the process standard, problem solving, are covered in the activities.

The questions and format are similar to those found on standardized math tests. The experience students gain from answering questions in this format may help increase their test scores.

These exercises can be used to enhance the regular math curriculum, to individualize instruction, to provide extra practice for home schoolers, or to review skills between grades.

The following math skills are covered in this book:

- **problem solving**
- **multiplication**
- **division**
- **integers**
- **fractions**
- **ratio and percent**
- **algebra**
- **polynomials**
- **graphing equations**
- **geometry**
- **probability & statistics**

Each **Math Achievement** book contains **four pretests in standardized test format** at the beginning of each book. The pretests have been designed so that they may be used individually, as four stand-alone tests, or in groups. They may be used to identify students' needs in specific areas, or to compare students' math abilities at the beginning and end of the school year. **A scoring box is also included on each activity page.** This scoring box can be programmed to suit your specific classroom and student needs with total problems, total correct, and score.

Read each problem. Circle the letter beside the correct answer.

Round amounts to the nearest dollar and estimate the cost of refreshments at a movie.

Popcorn	small	$1.49	Candy		55¢
	large	$2.29			
Soda	small	75¢	Ice Cream	small	55¢
	medium	$1.25		large	95¢
	large	$1.75			

1. How much would a small popcorn, candy, and a large soda cost?
    A. $4.50   B. $5.00   C. $3.50   D. $4.00

2. What would it cost to purchase a small soda, large soda, large popcorn, candy, and a small ice cream?
    A. $5.00   B. $6.00   C. $7.00   D. $4.50

3. Which is not a factor of 36?
    A.   5   B.   6   C.   3   D.   9

4. 4, 2, and 5 are all factors of which number?
    A.   115   B.   36   C.   85   D.   120

5. Find the least common multiple (LCM) of 4 and 6.
    A.   12   B.   24   C.   36   D.   48

6. Find the LCM of 3 and 6.
    A.   8   B.   18   C.   12   D.   6

7. 1 x 1 x 1 x 1 is the same as _____.
    A. 1^4 C. 4^2
    B.   4 x 1   D.   1 x 4

8. a^5 is the same as _____.
    A.   5 x a   C.   a x a x a x a x a
    B. 5^a D.   1 x 5

9. $\sqrt{16}$
    A.   16   C.   8
    B.   4   D.   2

10. $\sqrt{81}$
    A.   9   C.   18
    B.   12   D.   8

11. What is the absolute value of ⁻6?
    A.   ⁺6   B.   6   C.   ⁻6   D.   0

12. Simplify this expression: | ⁻4 | + | 3 | = _____.
    A.   1   B.   ⁻1   C.   ⁻7   D.   7

4

| Total Problems: | Total Correct: | Score: |

Read each problem. Circle the letter beside the correct answer.

1. $|12| - |^-2| =$ _____.
   A. 10   C. $^-1$
   B. 14   D. $^-14$

2. $|^-13| + |^-2| =$ _____.
   A. $^-15$ C. 15
   B. 11   D. $^-11$

3. $32 + (^-51) =$ _____.
   A. 19   C. 83
   B. $^-19$ D. $^-83$

4. $16 - (^-16) =$ _____.
   A. 0   C. 32
   B. $^-32$ D. 12

Express each decimal as a fraction or mixed number.

5. 0.75
   A. $7\frac{1}{2}$ B. $\frac{7}{10}$ C. $\frac{7}{8}$ D. $\frac{3}{4}$

6. 0.20
   A. $\frac{1}{5}$ B. $\frac{1}{10}$ C. $\frac{1}{2}$ D. $\frac{1}{4}$

7. 0.303
   A. $\frac{1}{3}$ B. $\frac{303}{1,000}$ C. $\frac{3}{10}$ D. $\frac{3}{4}$

8. 1.25
   A. $\frac{1}{5}$ B. $\frac{1}{10}$ C. $\frac{1}{2}$ D. $\frac{5}{4}$

9. A trash bag is 1.75 mills thick. This equals .00175 inches. What fraction of an inch is this?
   A. 175 thousandths   B. $1\frac{3}{4}$ C. 175 ten-thousandths   D. 175-hundred-thousandths

10. The Warriors won 30% of their football games last season. If they played 10 games, how many did they win?
    A. 9   B. 6   C. 3   D. 7

11. The Blue Devils will play 34 basketball games this year. If 17 are played at home, what percentage of the games are home games?
    A. 25%   B. 10%   C. 33%   D. 50%

12. At Robertson High School the bell rings at 8:05, 8:51, 8:55, and 9:41 each morning. When would the next bell ring?
    A. 10:30   B. 10:45   C. 10:31   D. 9:45

13. An apartment rents for $950 a month. The monthly rent is expected to increase $10 a month per year for the next 5 years. What will the monthly rent be in 5 years?
    A. $975   B. $1,000   C. $1,050   D. $900

14. Evaluate $a + b - 25$ if $a = 30$ and $b = 21$.
    A. 25   B. 29   C. 24   D. 26

Total Problems: _____   Total Correct: _____   Score: _____

Read each problem. Circle the letter beside the correct answer.

---

1. Evaluate $\frac{xy}{2}$ if $x = 3$ and $y = 6$.

     A.   9
     B.   5
     C.   4.5
     D.   18

2. Evaluate $\frac{12(x + y)}{2z + 3}$ if $x = 4$, $y = 5$, and $z = 3$.

     A.   15
     B.   10
     C.   18
     D.   12

---

3. Solve for v: $f = t + v$ if $f = 125$ and $t = 25$.

     A.   125
     B.   100
     C.   150
     D.   75

5. Solve for x: $x - (^-y) = z$ if $y = 4$ and $z = 10$.

     A.   7
     B.   4
     C.   6
     D.   8

4. Solve for b: $a + b = c$ if $a = 72$ and $c = 99$.

     A.   171
     B.   77
     C.   37
     D.   27

6. Solve for q: $p = q - r$ if $p = 38$ and $r = 50$.

     A.   88
     B.   58
     C. $^-12$
     D.   7

---

7. The formula for finding gas mileage is $M = \frac{d}{g}$, where M is miles per gallon, d is the distance traveled, and g is the number of gallons of gasoline used. Jerry's car gets 22 miles per gallon. How many gallons of gas does he need to travel 308 miles?

     A.   22   C.   14
     B.   12   D.   20

---

8. Will has $289.72 in his savings account. If it earns 6% annual interest, how much will it earn in 6 months?

     A. $16.40   C. $17.39
     B. $8.69   D. $9.38

---

9. The Pythagorean Theorem can be stated using the equation $a^2 + b^2 = c^2$.
Use the equation to find the value of c in this triangle when $a = 3$ in and $b = 4$ in.

     A.   5   C.   6
     B.   8   D.   9

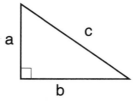

Total Problems:	Total Correct:	Score:

Read each problem. Circle the letter beside the correct answer.

Use the coordinate system to name the point for each ordered pair.

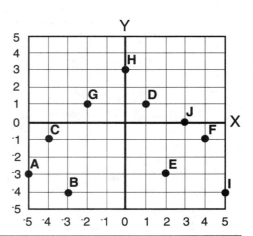

1. (⁻5, ⁻3)
   A. G   C. D
   B. J   D. A

2. (⁻3, ⁻4)
   A. E   C. B
   B. J   D. I

3. (1, 1)
   A. D   C. I
   B. A   D. B

4. (5, ⁻4)
   A. B   C. H
   B. F   D. I

5. The formula for finding the volume of a pyramid is $\frac{1}{3}$ Bh, where B is the area of base and h is the height. The base of this pyramid is a rectangle. The area of a rectangle is length x width. Find the volume of the pyramid.
   A. 79 cubic inches
   B. 84 cubic inches
   C. 56 cubic inches
   D. 86 cubic inches

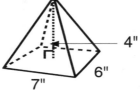

4"

6"

7"

Find the volume of each cylinder. Use the formula V = $\pi r^2 h$.

6. How much soil must Gus buy to fill a cylindrical planter 2 feet tall and 3 feet wide?
   A. 15 ft³
   B. 14.13 ft³
   C. 12.32 ft³
   D. 13.55 ft³

7. If Gus's planter is 2 feet wide and 2 feet tall, how much soil would he need?
   A. 6.28 ft³
   B. 12.55 ft³
   C. 13.14 ft³
   D. 8.28 ft³

Simplify each polynomial.

8. $2x^2 + x + 7x^2 - 4x$
   A. $5x^2 - 3x$ C. $9x^4 - 3$
   B. $9x^2 - 3x$ D. $3x^3 + 3x$

9. $(5x^2 + 4) - (4x^2 - 1)$
   A. $9x^2 - 3$ C. $x^2 + 3$
   B. $⁻9x^2 - 5$ D. $x^2 + 5$

10. Joanne has 3 new blouses and 4 new skirts that all coordinate. How many outfits can she make?
    A. 7   B. 14   C. 28   D. 12

Panel 1 (page 4)

Name _____   Pretest

Read each problem. Circle the letter beside the correct answer.

Round amounts to the nearest dollar and estimate the cost of refreshments at a movie.

Popcorn	small	$1.49	Candy		55¢
	large	$2.29			
Soda	small	75¢	Ice Cream	small	55¢
	medium	$1.25		large	95¢
	large	$1.75			

1. How much would a small popcorn, candy, and a large soda cost?
   A. $4.50   B. $5.00   C. $3.50   (D.) $4.00

2. What would it cost to purchase a small soda, large soda, large popcorn, candy, and a small ice cream?
   A. $5.00   (B.) $6.00   C. $7.00   D. $4.50

3. Which is not a factor of 36?
   (A.) 5   B. 6   C. 3   D. 9

4. 4, 2, and 5 are all factors of which number?
   A. 115   B. 36   C. 85   (D.) 120

5. Find the least common multiple (LCM) of 4 and 6.
   (A.) 12   B. 24   C. 36   D. 48

6. Find the LCM of 3 and 6.
   A. 8   B. 18   C. 12   (D.) 6

7. 1 x 1 x 1 x 1 is the same as _____.
   (A.) 1^4 C. 4^2
   B. 4 x 1   D. 1 x 4

8. a^5 is the same as _____.
   A. 5 x a   (C.) $a x a x a x a x a$
   B. 5^a D. 1 x 5

9. $\sqrt{16}$
   A. 16   C. 8
   (B.) 4   D. 2

10. $\sqrt{81}$
   (A.) 9   C. 18
   B. 12   D. 8

11. What is the absolute value of $^-6$?
   A. $^+6$ (B.) 6   C. $^-6$ D. 0

12. Simplify this expression: $|^-4| + |3| = $ _____.
   A. 1   B. $^-1$ C. $^-7$ (D.) 7

(4)   Total Problems: _____   Total Correct: _____   Score: _____   © Carson-Dellosa CD-2215

Panel 2 (page 5)

Name _____   Pretest

Read each problem. Circle the letter beside the correct answer.

1. $|12| - |^-2| = $ _____.
   (A.) 10   C. $^-1$
   B. 14   D. $^-14$

2. $|^-13| + |^-2| = $ _____.
   A. $^-15$ (C.) 15
   B. 11   D. $^-11$

3. $32 + (^-51) = $ _____.
   A. 19   C. 83
   (B.) $^-19$ D. $^-83$

4. $16 - (^-16) = $ _____.
   A. 0   (C.) 32
   B. $^-32$ D. 12

Express each decimal as a fraction or mixed number.

5. 0.75
   A. $7\frac{1}{2}$ B. $\frac{7}{10}$ C. $\frac{7}{8}$ (D.) $\frac{3}{4}$

6. 0.20
   (A.) $\frac{1}{5}$ B. $\frac{1}{10}$ C. $\frac{1}{2}$ D. $\frac{1}{4}$

7. 0.303
   A. $\frac{1}{3}$ (B.) $\frac{303}{1,000}$ C. $\frac{3}{10}$ D. $\frac{3}{4}$

8. 1.25
   A. $\frac{1}{5}$ B. $\frac{1}{10}$ C. $\frac{1}{2}$ (D.) $\frac{5}{4}$

9. A trash bag is 1.75 mills thick. This equals .00175 inches. What fraction of an inch is this?
   A. 175 thousandths   B. $1\frac{3}{4}$ C. 175 ten-thousandths   (D.) 175 hundred-thousandths

10. The Warriors won 30% of their football games last season. If they played 10 games, how many did they win?
   A. 9   B. 6   (C.) 3   D. 7

11. The Blue Devils will play 34 basketball games this year. If 17 are played at home, what percentage of the games are home games?
   A. 25%   B. 10%   C. 33%   (D.) 50%

12. At Robertson High School the bell rings at 8:05, 8:51, 8:55, and 9:41 each morning. When would the next bell ring?
   A. 10:30   B. 10:45   C. 10:31   (D.) 9:45

13. An apartment rents for $950 a month. The monthly rent is expected to increase $10 a month per year for the next 5 years. What will the monthly rent be in 5 years?
   A. $975   (B.) $1,000   C. $1,050   D. $900

14. Evaluate $a + b - 25$ if $a = 30$ and $b = 21$.
   A. 25   B. 29   C. 24   (D.) 26

© Carson-Dellosa CD-2215   Total Problems: _____   Total Correct: _____   Score: _____   (5)

Panel 3 (page 6)

Name _____   Pretest

Read each problem. Circle the letter beside the correct answer.

1. Evaluate $\frac{xy}{2}$ if $x = 3$ and $y = 6$.
   (A.) 9
   B. 5
   C. 4.5
   D. 18

2. Evaluate $\frac{12(x + y)}{2z + 3}$ if $x = 4, y = 5$, and $z = 3$.
   A. 15
   B. 10
   C. 18
   (D.) 12

3. Solve for v: $f = t + v$ if $f = 125$ and $t = 25$.
   A. 125
   (B.) 100
   C. 150
   D. 75

4. Solve for b: $a + b = c$ if $a = 72$ and $c = 99$.
   A. 171
   B. 77
   C. 37
   (D.) 27

5. Solve for x: $x - (^-y) = z$ if $y = 4$ and $z = 10$.
   A. 7
   B. 4
   (C.) 6
   D. 8

6. Solve for q: $p = q - r$ if $p = 38$ and $r = 50$.
   (A.) 88
   B. 58
   C. $^-12$
   D. 7

7. The formula for finding gas mileage is $M = \frac{d}{g}$, where M is miles per gallon, d is the distance traveled, and g is the number of gallons of gasoline used. Jerry's car gets 22 miles per gallon. How many gallons of gas does he need to travel 308 miles?
   A. 22   (C.) 14
   B. 12   D. 20

8. Will has $289.72 in his savings account. If it earns 6% annual interest, how much will it earn in 6 months?
   A. $16.40   C. $17.39
   (B.) $8.69   D. $9.38

9. The Pythagorean Theorem can be stated using the equation $a^2 + b^2 = c^2$.
   Use the equation to find the value of c in this triangle when $a = 3$ in. and $b = 4$ in.
   (A.) 5   C. 6
   B. 8   D. 9

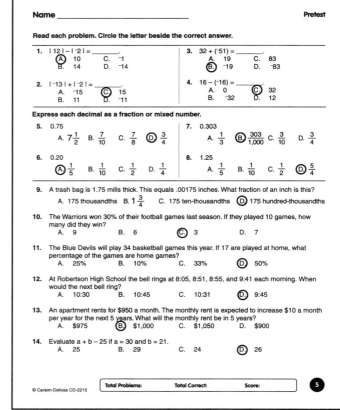

(6)   Total Problems: _____   Total Correct: _____   Score: _____   © Carson-Dellosa CD-2215

Panel 4 (page 7)

Name _____   Pretest

Read each problem. Circle the letter beside the correct answer.

Use the coordinate system to name the point for each ordered pair.

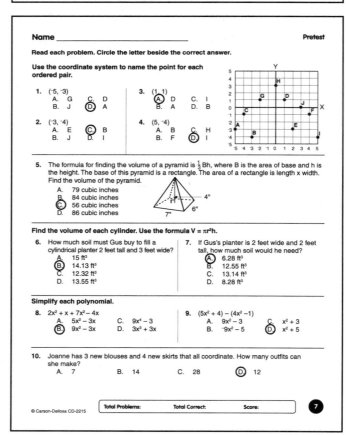

1. ($^-5, ^-3$)
   A. G   C. D
   B. J   (D.) A

2. ($^-3, ^-4$)
   A. E   (C.) B
   B. J   D. I

3. (1, 1)
   (A.) D   C. I
   B. A   D. B

4. (5, $^-4$)
   A. B   C. H
   B. F   (D.) I

5. The formula for finding the volume of a pyramid is $\frac{1}{3}Bh$, where B is the area of base and h is the height. The base of this pyramid is a rectangle. The area of a rectangle is length x width. Find the volume of the pyramid.
   A. 79 cubic inches
   B. 84 cubic inches
   (C.) 56 cubic inches
   D. 86 cubic inches

Find the volume of each cylinder. Use the formula $V = \pi r^2 h$.

6. How much soil must Gus buy to fill a cylindrical planter 2 feet tall and 3 feet wide?
   A. 15 ft³
   (B.) 14.13 ft³
   C. 12.32 ft³
   D. 13.55 ft³

7. If Gus's planter is 2 feet wide and 2 feet tall, how much soil would he need?
   (A.) 6.28 ft³
   B. 12.55 ft³
   C. 13.14 ft³
   D. 8.28 ft³

Simplify each polynomial.

8. $2x^2 + x + 7x^2 - 4x$
   A. $5x^2 - 3x$ C. $9x^4 - 3$
   (B.) $9x^2 - 3x$ D. $3x^3 + 3x$

9. $(5x^2 + 4) - (4x^2 - 1)$
   A. $9x^2 - 3$ C. $x^2 + 3$
   B. $^-9x^2 - 5$ (D.) $x^2 + 5$

10. Joanne has 3 new blouses and 4 new skirts that all coordinate. How many outfits can she make?
   A. 7   B. 14   C. 28   (D.) 12

© Carson-Dellosa CD-2215   Total Problems: _____   Total Correct: _____   Score: _____   (7)

Study the box below. On the line provided, write the first 5 nonzero multiples of each number.

Rule:	Example:
The product of two whole numbers is a multiple of those numbers.	The first 5 nonzero multiples of 3 are: 3 x 1 = **3**, 3 x 2 = **6**, 3 x 3 = **9**, 3 x 4 = **12**, and 3 x 5 = **15**.

1. 9 _____

2. 6 _____

3. 11 _____

4. 25 _____

5. 12 _____

6. 21 _____

7. 50 _____

8. 100 _____

Study the box below. List all of the factors of the given number.

Rule:	Example:
A factor is a number that is multiplied by another number to give a product.	16 = 1 x 16, 2 x 8, 4 x 4 factors = **1, 2, 4, 8, 16**

9. 36 _____

10. 75 _____

11. 63 _____

12. 49 _____

13. 84 _____

14. 90 _____

15. 42 _____

16. 56 _____

Total Problems:	Total Correct:	Score:

Study the box below. In the space provided, make a factor tree to find the prime factorization of each number. Express the prime factorization using exponents.

Rule:

When a number is expressed as the product of all prime numbers, the expression is called **prime factorization**. A prime number has only two factors, 1 and the number itself. A **composite number** has more than two factors.

Example:

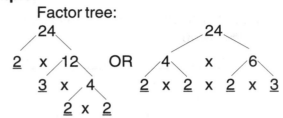

Factor tree:

The prime factorization of 24 is **2 • 2 • 2 • 3**. Using exponents, it would be written $2^3 • 3$.

1. 60

4. 9

2. 81

5. 39

3. 135

6. 150

Total Problems:	Total Correct:	Score:

Name _____

Study the box below. Find the greatest common factor (GCF) for each set of numbers. Write the answer in the space provided.

Rule:	**Example:**
List all of the factors of each number.	18, 24
Then, find the greatest factor common to both numbers. This will be the greatest common factor (GCF).	18: 1, 2, 3, ⑥ 9, 18
	24: 1, 2, 3, 4, ⑥ 8, 12, 24
	GCF = 6

1. 56, 84

2. 8, 9

3. 14, 42

4. 48, 84

5. 78, 91

6. 40, 60

7. 18, 30, 42

8. 45, 60, 120

9. 15, 35, 70

10. $10ab, 25b^2$

11. $16x, 40x^2$

12. $9mn, 15m^2, 24mn^2$

| **Total Problems:** | **Total Correct:** | **Score:** |

Name _____

Study the box below. Find the least common multiple (LCM) of each set of numbers. Write the answer in the space provided.

Rule:	Example:
List the multiples of each number.	8, 12
Stop when you have found the smallest multiple common of both numbers. This will be the least common multiple (LCM).	8: 8, 16, (24)
	12: 12, (24)
	LCM = 24

1. 10, 14

6. 10, 25

11. 7, 21, 84

2. 24, 36

7. 12, 16

12. 3, 5, 7

3. 18, 72

8. 18, 32

13. 10cd, 40d

4. 2, 5, 8

9. 15, 24

14. 3y, $15y^2$, 30

5. 32, 64

10. 9, 12, 15

15. $4x^2$, 5x

Total Problems: **Total Correct:**   **Score:**

Study the box below. Follow the directions and write the answer in the space provided.

Rule:	**Examples:**
An exponent tells the number of times a base is multiplied by itself.	$4^3 = 4 \cdot 4 \cdot 4$ Expanded form
$9 \cdot 9 \cdot 9 \cdot 9 = 9^4$ exponent base	$2 \cdot 4 \cdot 2 \cdot 4 = 2^2 \cdot 4^2$ Exponential form
	$5^2 = 25$ Simplified

Write each problem in expanded form.

1. 7^6

2. 4^5

3. x^3

4. $a^2 \cdot b^2$

5. $8^9 \cdot 9$

6. $2^2 \cdot 3^5$

Write each problem in exponential form.

7. $5 \cdot 5$

8. $11 \cdot 11 \cdot 11$

9. $6 \cdot 6 \cdot 6$

10. $10 \cdot 9 \cdot 9 \cdot 10$

11. $2 \cdot 2 \cdot 4 \cdot 3 \cdot 3$

12. $3 \cdot 2 \cdot 3$

13. $m \cdot n \cdot m \cdot m$

14. $x \cdot y \cdot x \cdot y$

15. $a \cdot a \cdot a$

Simplify each problem.

16. 7^2

17. $4^4 + 3$

18. $2^5 \cdot 3^2 \cdot 4^3$

19. $8^2 \cdot 3^2$

20. $12^2 + 9^2$

21. $4^2 \cdot 6^3 \cdot 8^0$

Total Problems:	Total Correct:	Score:	**13**

Name _____

Study the box below. Simplify. Write the answers in exponent form in the space provided.

Rules:	Examples:
To multiply powers with like bases, add the exponents. Use the sum as the exponent with the base.	$4^4 \cdot 4^5 = 4^{4+5} = \mathbf{4^9}$
To divide powers with like bases, subtract the exponents. Use the difference as the exponent with the base.	$\dfrac{3^6}{3^2} = 3^{6-2} = \mathbf{3^4}$

1. $2^3 \cdot 2^5$

2. $5^8 \cdot 5^2$

3. $8^3 \cdot 8^4$

4. $\dfrac{10^3}{10}$

5. $\dfrac{7^5}{7^4}$

6. $\dfrac{6^4}{6^2}$

7. $4^2 \cdot 4^2$

8. $9^2 \cdot 9 \cdot 9^3$

9. $3 \cdot 3^4 \cdot 3^3$

10. $\dfrac{5^4}{5^4}$

11. $\dfrac{11^8}{11^5}$

12. $\dfrac{4^3}{4^2}$

13. $x^3 \cdot x^6$

14. $m \cdot m^3 \cdot m^4$

15. $c^5 \cdot c^2$

16. $\dfrac{y^5}{y^4}$

17. $\dfrac{a^7}{a^4}$

18. $\dfrac{b^5}{b^4}$

Total Problems: _____ Total Correct: _____ Score: _____

Name _____

Scientific Notation and
Standard Form

Study the box below. Express each number in scientific notation. Write the answer in the space provided.

Rule:	Examples:
Scientific notation expresses numbers using powers of 10.	$301,000 = \mathbf{3.01 \times 10^5}$
Change the number (n) by moving the decimal point so that $1 \leq n < 10$.	$0.00532 = \mathbf{5.32 \times 10^{-3}}$
Count the number of places the decimal point was moved. That number will become the power of 10 (positive if the decimal point moved to the left, negative if it moved to the right).	

1. 0.000091

2. 2,700,000

3. 450,000,000

4. 0.0000008

5. 0.00083

6. 72,000,000

7. 65,000

8. 402,000

9. 0.000000063

Express each number in standard form.

Rule:	Examples:
Identify the power on the 10.	$9 \times 10^6 = \mathbf{9,000,000}$
For a postive power, move the decimal point that many places to the right.	$2.1 \times 10^{-6} = \mathbf{0.0000021}$
For a negative power, move the decimal point that many places to the left.	

10. 7.15×10^4

11. 3.52×10^{-6}

12. 5×10^{-8}

13. 1.28×10

14. 8.72×10^{-10}

15. 2.6×10^{-3}

16. 4.3×10^7

17. 6.4×10^{-5}

18. 4×10^{-7}

Total Problems: _____ Total Correct: _____ Score: _____

Study the box below. Find the square of each number. Write the answer in the space provided.

Rule:	Example:
To find the square of a number, multiply it by itself.	$8^2 = 8 \times 8 = \mathbf{64}$

1. 5^2 _____

2. 7^2 _____

3. 2^2 _____

4. 1^2 _____

5. 3^2 _____

6. 12^2 _____

7. 21^2 _____

8. 6^2 _____

9. 15^2 _____

10. 18^2 _____

11. 10^2 _____

12. 24^2 _____

13. 13^2 _____

14. 20^2 _____

15. 16^2 _____

Study the box below. Find each square root. Write the answer in the space provided.

Rule:	Example:
A radical sign, $\sqrt{}$, is the symbol used to indicate a nonnegative square root.	$\sqrt{16} = \mathbf{4}$ Since $4^2 = 16$, 4 is the square root of 16.

16. $\sqrt{81}$

17. $\sqrt{36}$

18. $\sqrt{9}$

19. $\sqrt{169}$

20. $\sqrt{1}$

21. $\sqrt{196}$

22. $\sqrt{324}$

23. $\sqrt{225}$

24. $\sqrt{100}$

25. $\sqrt{361}$

26. $\sqrt{625}$

27. $\sqrt{256}$

28. $\sqrt{289}$

29. $\sqrt{0.16}$

30. $\sqrt{0.04}$

Total Problems: _____   Total Correct: _____   Score: _____

Study the box below. Find the value of each expression. Write the answer on the line provided.

Rule:	Examples:	
Order of Operations: 1. Work inside all grouping symbols. 2. Compute all exponents. 3. Multiply and divide from left to right. 4. Add and subtract from left to right.	$24 - 2^2 \bullet 3$ $24 - 4 \bullet 3$ $24 - 12$ **12**	$2 \bullet (3 + 5) - 7$ $2 \bullet 8 - 7$ $16 - 7$ **9**

1. $12 \div 4 + 12 \div 3$

2. $21 \div 3 + 4 \bullet 9$

3. $27 \div 3^2 + 5$

4. $6 \bullet 3 \div 2 - 1$

5. $(9 + 6) \div 3$

6. $9 + 6 \div 3$

7. $76 - 7 \bullet 2^3$

8. $(16 - 7) \bullet 2$

9. $24 \div 4 - 3 \bullet 2$

10. $(10 - 2)^2 \bullet 2$

11. $10 - 2^2 \bullet 2$

12. $2^2 \bullet 10 \div 5 + 3$

13. $2[6(9 - 3)] - 20$

14. $6[(9 + 5) - 2(3)]$

15. $(8 - 5)^2 + 9 \div 3$

16. $\dfrac{46 - 4}{7}$

17. $\dfrac{16 + 8}{2^2}$

18. $\dfrac{27 \div 3}{3^2}$

Total Problems: _____ Total Correct: _____ Score: _____

Solve each problem. Show your work and write the answer in the space provided.

---

1. For each problem below, insert parentheses to make each sentence true.
   A. $15 \div 21 - 16 + 7 = 10$

   B. $30 \div 6 \cdot 5 = 1$

   C. $6 \div 2 + 5 \cdot 4 = 23$

5. Write 8^2 as a power of 2.

---

2. Alex is 16 years old. The GCF of his age and his younger sister's age is 8. How old is his younger sister?

6. Solve for x.
   A. $m^{x+5} = m^3 m^5$

   B. $m^{x-5} = m^6 m^4$

   C. $m^{3x} = m^2 m^4$

---

3. Mr. King goes to the laundromat every eighth day. Ms. Simon goes every sixth day. If they are both there on March 1, on what date will they both be back in the laundromat together?

7. Multiply. Express each answer in scientific notation.
   A. $(2.5 \times 10^5)(4 \times 10^3)$

   B. $(4.1 \times 10^{-4})(6 \times 10^{-5})$

   C. $(3 \times 10^2)(5.1 \times 10^7)$

---

4. Choose nonzero whole numbers for x, y, and z to make the following true:
   $$\sqrt{x} \cdot \sqrt{y} = \sqrt{z}$$

8. The population of a large country was estimated to be 5.5×10^6. The population of a small country was estimated to be 3.4×10^4. Approximately how many more people live in the larger country than the smaller one? Express your answer in scientific notation.

18

| Total Problems: | Total Correct: | Score: |

Study the box below. Graph each set of numbers on a number line in the space provided.

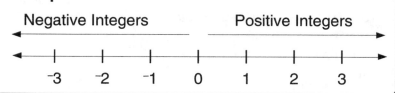

Rule:	**Example:**
An **integer** is a whole number, a negative whole number, or 0.	Negative Integers Positive Integers ⁻3 ⁻2 ⁻1 0 1 2 3

1. {0, 2, ⁻2}

2. {1, ⁻3, 4}

3. {6, ⁻4, ⁻1}

4. {⁻2, ⁻5, ⁻3}

Study the box below. Find the absolute value and write the answer on the line provided.

Rule:	**Example:**
Absolute value is the distance a number is from 0 on the number line. The following symbol is used when asked to find the absolute value: | |.	| ⁻10 | = **10** ⁻10 is 10 places from 0 on the number line, so the absolute value of ⁻10 is 10.

5. \| ⁻7 \| _____   **8.** \| 18 \| _____   **11.** \| 26 \| _____   **14.** \| 14 − 9 \| ____

6. \| 12 \| _____   **9.** \| 0 \| _____   **12.** \| 37 \| _____   **15.** \| 20 + 8 \| ____

7. \| ⁻9 \| _____   **10.** \| ⁻4 \| _____   **13.** \| ⁻15 \| _____   **16.** \| 17 − 8 \| ____

Total Problems: _____   Total Correct: _____   Score: _____   **19**

Study the box below. Compare using <, >, or =. Write the answer in the box provided.

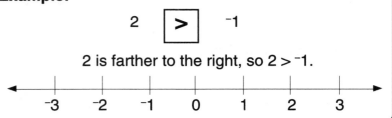

Rule:

You can use a number line to compare integers. Values increase as you move to the right on the number line.

Example:

2   >   ⁻1

2 is farther to the right, so 2 > ⁻1.

1. 15 ☐ ⁻17

2. ⁻81 ☐ ⁻18

3. ⁻21 ☐ ⁻22

4. 63 ☐ ⁻67

5. 40 ☐ ⁻40

6. ⁻38 ☐ ⁻148

7. ⁻51 ☐ ⁻41

8. ⁻19 ☐ ⁻19

9. ⁻242 ☐ ⁻24

10. ⁻72 ☐ ⁻71

11. ⁻33 ☐ ⁻34

12. ⁻91 ☐ ⁻94

Order the numbers in each set from least to greatest. Write the answer on the line provided.

13. {⁻9, ⁻12, ⁻7}

_____

14. {14, 0, ⁻14}

_____

15. {⁻50, ⁻75, ⁻45, ⁻60}

_____

16. {13, ⁻20, ⁻57, 82, ⁻32}

_____

17. {60, ⁻60, ⁻20, 20, 0, 10}

_____

18. {⁻300, 300, ⁻250, 100, ⁻130}

_____

Total Problems: Total Correct: Score:

Study the box below. Find each sum. Write the answer in the space provided.

Rules:	Examples:	
The sum of two postive integers is positive.	$19 + 5 = \mathbf{24}$	$^-12 + 15$
The sum of two negative integers is negative.	$^-11 + {}^-10 = \mathbf{^-21}$	$\mid {}^-12 \mid = 12$
When one integer is postive and one integer is negative, subtract the smaller absolute value from the larger absolute value. Give the result the sign of the integer with the greater absolute value.		$\mid 15 \mid = 15$
		$15 - 12 = 3$
		$^-12 + 15 = \mathbf{3}$

1. $14 + (^-7)$

2. $(^-20) + (^-5)$

3. $(^-18) + (^-4)$

4. $^-9 + 25$

5. $15 + (^-31)$

6. $^-20 + 7$

7. $^-31 + (^-53)$

8. $47 + 63$

9. $14 + (^-22) + 45$

10. $^-37 + (^-51) + 24$

11. $^-27 + 41 + 16$

12. $71 + (^-71)$

13. $51 + (^-12 + {}^-12)$

14. $^-25 + 5 + (^-10)$

15. $^-14 + 14 + 63$

16. $^-17 + 16 + (^-15)$

17. $^-27 + 31 + (^-19)$

18. $41 + (^-41) + 41$

Name _____

Study the box below. Subtract. Write the answer on the line provided.

Rule:	Examples:	
To subtract an integer, add its opposite.	⁻15 – (⁻9) ⁻15 + 9 = **⁻6**	⁻14 – 21 ⁻14 + ⁻21 = **⁻35**

1. ⁻7 – 15 _____

2. 14 – 20 _____

3. ⁻15 – 10 _____

4. 18 – 21 _____

5. 37 – (⁻14) _____

6. 17 – 15 _____

7. ⁻11 – 6 _____

8. 13 – 27 _____

9. 40 – (⁻14) _____

10. ⁻35 – 35 _____

11. ⁻35 – (⁻35) _____

12. 15 – (⁻20) _____

13. 31 – (⁻15) _____

14. 28 – (⁻18) _____

15. ⁻36 – 20 _____

16. 33 – (⁻16) _____

17. ⁻57 – 27 _____

18. ⁻43 – 22 _____

19. ⁻17 – (⁻30) _____

20. ⁻73 – 63 _____

21. 90 – (⁻1) _____

22. ⁻58 – 58 _____

23. 61 – (⁻61) _____

24. 46 – (⁻56) _____

22

Total Problems:	Total Correct:	Score:

Name _____

Study the box below. Find each product or quotient. Write the answer on the line provided.

Rules:	Examples:		
The product or quotient of two integers with the same sign is positive.	⁻5 • ⁻8 = **40**	4 • ⁻4 = ⁻**16**	(100 ÷ ⁻5) • ⁻2
The product or quotient of two integers with different signs is negative.	24 ÷ 6 = **4**	⁻72 ÷ 8 = ⁻**9**	(⁻20) • ⁻2 = **40**

1. ⁻9 • ⁻6 _____

2. ⁻16 ÷ ⁻8 _____

3. ⁻7 • ⁻3 _____

4. ⁻63 ÷ 9 _____

5. ⁻7 • 28 _____

6. ⁻54 • ⁻2 _____

7. 124 ÷ ⁻4 _____

8. 24 • ⁻5 _____

9. ⁻2 • 17 _____

10. ⁻144 ÷ 12 _____

11. 288 ÷ ⁻18 _____

12. 0 • ⁻43 _____

13. ⁻8 • ⁻45 _____

14. 10 • ⁻6 _____

15. 208 ÷ ⁻26 _____

16. 10 • 46 _____

17. ⁻312 ÷ ⁻24 _____

18. (7 • ⁻7) • ⁻2 _____

19. (⁻132 ÷ 11) • 4 _____

20. ⁻5(⁻3)(6) _____

Total Problems: _____   Total Correct: _____   Score: _____

Solve each problem. Show your work and write the answer in the space provided.

1. Complete the following:
   A. The opposite of a negative integer is a _____ integer.
   B. The integer _____ is neither a positive nor negative integer.
   C. The absolute value of a nonzero integer is always a _____ integer.

2. Find two values for y that make this sentence true: $|y| = 5$.

3. Read the sentences below. Then, use the numbers and $<$ or $>$ symbols to write two inequalities for each sentence.
   A. Water boils at 212°F. It freezes at 32°F.

   B. Yesterday's high temperature was 12°F. The low temperature was ⁻5°F.

4. Tell whether each sum is positive, negative, or zero.
   A. x and y are positive.
      x + y is _____ .
   B. x is positive; y is negative.
      −x + y is _____ .
   C. x = y; x and y are negative.
      x ÷ (⁻y) is _____ .

5. Write five addition sentences whose sum is ⁻4.

6. Mrs. Riddle has $543.73 in her checking account. She writes a check for $840.00. By how much has she overdrawn her account?

7. An elevator went up 3 floors, down 6 floors, up 7 floors, down 9 floors, and up 8 floors. It stopped on the 32ⁿᵈ floor. On what floor did the elevator start?

Total Problems: _____   Total Correct: _____   Score: _____

Name _____

Study the box below. Reduce each fraction to lowest terms. Write the answer in the space provided.

Rule:	Example:
To reduce a fraction to lowest terms, divide the numerator and denominator by their greatest common factor (GCF).	$\dfrac{20 \div 5}{25 \div 5} = \dfrac{4}{5}$

1. $\dfrac{18}{36} =$

2. $\dfrac{12}{20} =$

3. $\dfrac{28}{48} =$

4. $\dfrac{17}{51} =$

5. $\dfrac{9}{24} =$

6. $\dfrac{16}{64} =$

7. $\dfrac{49}{140} =$

8. $\dfrac{52}{56} =$

9. $\dfrac{3}{30} =$

10. $\dfrac{70}{105} =$

11. $\dfrac{60}{125} =$

12. $\dfrac{45}{72} =$

13. $\dfrac{6}{15} =$

14. $\dfrac{15}{80} =$

15. $\dfrac{78}{112} =$

16. $\dfrac{34}{60} =$

17. $\dfrac{12}{90} =$

18. $\dfrac{124}{172} =$

19. $\dfrac{88}{121} =$

20. $\dfrac{11}{99} =$

21. $\dfrac{144}{216} =$

22. $\dfrac{245}{428} =$

23. $\dfrac{105}{133} =$

24. $\dfrac{42}{91} =$

Total Problems: _____   Total Correct: _____   Score: _____

Study the examples below. Round each fraction to the nearest whole number or one-half. Write the answer in the space provided.

Examples:

$1\frac{1}{8} = 1$	$2\frac{3}{5} = 2\frac{1}{2}$	$4\frac{12}{13} = 5$
The numerator is much smaller that the denominator, so round down to the nearest whole number.	The numerator is about half of the denominator, so round to the nearest one-half.	The numerator and denominator are close in value, so round up to the nearest whole number.

1. $3\frac{18}{36} =$

3. $3\frac{3}{17} =$

5. $3\frac{7}{8} =$

7. $7\frac{1}{9} =$

2. $8\frac{1}{15} =$

4. $6\frac{4}{9} =$

6. $4\frac{7}{18} =$

8. $9\frac{9}{11} =$

Study the box below. Estimate each sum or difference. Write the answer in the space provided.

Rule:	**Example:**
To estimate a sum or difference, round each fraction to the nearest whole number or one-half. Then, add or subtract.	$3\frac{4}{7} + 5\frac{1}{11} =$ $\downarrow \qquad \downarrow$ $3\frac{1}{2} + 5 = 8\frac{1}{2}$

9. $6\frac{1}{5} - 3\frac{6}{7} =$

11. $4\frac{3}{8} - \frac{1}{10} =$

13. $8\frac{1}{15} - 4\frac{2}{3} =$

10. $5\frac{3}{4} + 7\frac{7}{8} =$

12. $9\frac{1}{9} + 3\frac{3}{7} =$

14. $6\frac{5}{8} - 4\frac{1}{12} =$

Total Problems: **Total Correct:**   **Score:**

Study the box below. Find each sum or difference and reduce to lowest terms. Write the answer in the space provided.

Rule:

1. Change any mixed or whole number to an improper fraction.

2. Rewrite each fraction using the least common denominator (LCD).

3. Add or subtract. Reduce if necessary.

Example:

$$^-2\frac{1}{2} = \frac{^-5}{2} = \frac{^-25}{10}$$
$$+ \ 3\frac{1}{5} = + \frac{16}{5} = + \frac{32}{10}$$
$$\frac{7}{10}$$

1. $2\frac{1}{2}$
   $-\ \ \frac{1}{3}$

3. $^-5\frac{7}{8}$
   $-\ 2\frac{5}{6}$

5. $3\frac{5}{12}$
   $+\ 2\frac{1}{3}$

7. $\frac{9}{10}$
   $+\ 2\frac{1}{3}$

2. $4\frac{3}{8}$
   $-\ 2\frac{1}{4}$

4. $^-1\frac{7}{8}$
   $+\ \ \frac{7}{12}$

6. $4\frac{3}{10}$
   $-\ 3\frac{1}{2}$

8. $12\frac{1}{5}$
   $-11\frac{7}{8}$

9. $3\frac{5}{8} - (^-2\frac{3}{5}) =$

11. $12\frac{5}{8} - (^-3\frac{2}{5}) =$

10. $3\frac{7}{10} + (^-3\frac{7}{10}) =$

12. $2\frac{1}{2} + (^-3\frac{2}{7}) =$

Total Problems: **Total Correct:**   **Score:**

Name _____

Study the box below. Find each product and reduce to lowest terms. Write the answer in the space provided.

Rule:	**Example:**
1. Change each mixed number or whole number to an improper fraction. If a numerator or denominator share a common factor, "cancel" by dividing the numerator and denominator by that factor. 2. Multiply the numerators. 3. Multiply the denominators.	$4 \times 2\frac{1}{2} =$ $\frac{\overset{2}{\cancel{4}}}{1} \times \frac{5}{\underset{1}{\cancel{2}}} = \frac{10}{1} = \mathbf{10}$

1. $\frac{1}{7} \times \frac{1}{8} =$

2. $4\frac{1}{2} \times 8 =$

3. $\frac{3}{4} \times \frac{8}{9} =$

4. $5 \times \frac{1}{10} =$

5. $7\frac{7}{8} \times \frac{5}{9} =$

6. $1\frac{1}{9} \times \frac{27}{40} =$

7. $3 \times 1\frac{2}{3} =$

8. $^{-}5 \times 2\frac{3}{4} =$

9. $4\frac{1}{2} \times \left(\frac{3}{4}\right)^2 =$

10. $2\frac{2}{3} \times 2\frac{1}{5} =$

11. $^{-}3 \times \left(\frac{2}{5}\right)^2 =$

12. $^{-}2\frac{5}{6} \times 4\frac{2}{3} =$

13. $\frac{2}{3} \times \frac{3}{4} \times \frac{2}{5} =$

14. $2\frac{1}{4} \times 4 \times \frac{1}{3} =$

15. $\frac{^{-}5}{2} \times \frac{5}{3} \times \frac{3}{5} =$

Total Problems:	Total Correct:	Score:

Study the box below. Find each quotient and reduce to lowest terms. Write the answer in the space provided.

Rule:	**Example:**
1. Write any mixed or whole numbers as improper fractions. 2. Multiply by the multiplicative inverse (reciprocal).	$^-15 \div \dfrac{3}{5}$ $\dfrac{^-15}{1} \div \dfrac{3}{5}$ $\dfrac{^-15}{1} \times \dfrac{5}{3} = \dfrac{^-45}{3} = {}^-15$

1. $\dfrac{3}{4} \div 9 =$

2. $\dfrac{6}{7} \div \dfrac{3}{8} =$

3. $\dfrac{5}{12} \div \dfrac{4}{15} =$

4. $^-7\dfrac{1}{3} \div 1\dfrac{2}{9} =$

5. $5 \div \dfrac{^-1}{4} =$

6. $\dfrac{15}{8} \div {}^-3 =$

7. $^-5\dfrac{2}{7} \div \dfrac{3}{8} =$

8. $^-7\dfrac{3}{5} \div {}^-1\dfrac{9}{10} =$

9. $5\dfrac{1}{3} \div {}^-2\dfrac{2}{3} =$

10. $4 \div {}^-6\dfrac{2}{3} =$

11. $\dfrac{14}{11} \div \dfrac{16}{22} =$

12. $\dfrac{5}{7} \div 5\dfrac{1}{14} =$

13. $^-1\dfrac{1}{2} \div \dfrac{3}{20} =$

14. $^-2 \div \dfrac{^-1}{3} =$

15. $^-3\dfrac{1}{4} \div 2\dfrac{1}{6} =$

Name _____

Solve each word problem. Show your work and write the answer in the space provided.

---

1. Diane needs to purchase $1\frac{1}{2}$ yards of fabric for a shirt she is sewing and $3\frac{1}{2}$ yards of fabric for a sports jacket she is sewing. How many yards does she need in all?

5. Sherry's mother told her she needed to roast her turkey $\frac{1}{4}$ hour for each pound. If she purchased a $13\frac{1}{2}$-pound turkey, how long would she have to roast it?

2. At the track meet, Jeremy cleared 4 feet $4\frac{1}{4}$ inches. Ronnie jumped $1\frac{1}{2}$ inches higher. How high did Ronnie jump?

6. A recipe for a dozen muffins calls for $2\frac{1}{2}$ cups of flour. How much flour is needed to make half a dozen muffins?

3. A unit fraction is a fraction that has a numerator of 1. Express $\frac{1}{3}$ as the sum of three unit fractions.

7. Katrina purchased a wooden board that was 18 feet long. If she needs to cut it into pieces that are 2 feet 6 inches long, how many pieces can be cut from the board?

4. Marcus is typing a paper for his English class. The top margin must be a $\frac{1}{2}$ inch and the bottom margin must be $\frac{3}{4}$ inch. If the paper is 11 inches long, what is the length of the page inside the margin?

8. Ronald is putting up a fence in his backyard. Each section of the fence is $5\frac{1}{2}$ feet long. If he installs 6 sections, how much fence has been installed?

Total Problems: _____   Total Correct: _____   Score: _____

Study the box below. Use cross products to determine whether each pair of ratios is equal. Write "yes" or "no" on the line provided.

Rule:	Example:
A ratio is a comparison of two numbers. Cross multiply. If the cross products are equal, then the ratios are equal.	$\frac{2}{3}$, $\frac{8}{12}$ 2 x 12 = 24 $\frac{2}{3}$ ✗ $\frac{8}{12}$ 8 x 3 = 24 24 = 24, so, **yes, the ratios are equal.**

1. $\frac{4}{16}$, $\frac{8}{20}$ _____

2. $\frac{21}{28}$, $\frac{3}{4}$ _____

3. $\frac{21}{49}$, $\frac{6}{14}$ _____

4. $\frac{6}{15}$, $\frac{3}{7}$ _____

5. $\frac{16}{17}$, $\frac{8}{9}$ _____

6. $\frac{12}{15}$, $\frac{4}{5}$ _____

7. $\frac{3}{11}$, $\frac{9}{33}$ _____

8. $\frac{2}{5}$, $\frac{14}{25}$ _____

9. $\frac{2.1}{7}$, $\frac{1.4}{3.8}$ _____

Study the box below. Express each rate as a unit rate. Round answers to the nearest tenth. Write the answer on the line provided.

Rules:	Examples:
A **rate** is simply a ratio of two measurements with different units. A **unit rate** is a rate in which the denominator is 1.	rate: **$63 / 7 hours** unit rate: $63 ÷ 7 = **$9 / 1 hour**

10. 1,150 words / 5 minutes _____

11. 30 days / 5 weeks _____

12. 550 miles / 9 hours _____

13. $.60 / 4 apples _____

Name _____

Study the box below. Solve each proportion. Write the answer in the space provided.

Rule:	Example:
A **proportion** is two equivalent ratios. Cross products can be used to solve proportions.	$\dfrac{x}{27} = \dfrac{8}{6}$ $6 \cdot x = 27 \cdot 8$ $6x = 216$ $x = 216 \div 6$ **$x = 36$**

1. $\dfrac{4}{12} = \dfrac{y}{9}$

2. $\dfrac{7}{16} = \dfrac{x}{32}$

3. $\dfrac{9}{27} = \dfrac{5}{b}$

4. $\dfrac{6}{x} = \dfrac{18}{24}$

5. $\dfrac{4}{7} = \dfrac{x}{21}$

6. $\dfrac{n}{2} = \dfrac{6}{15}$

7. $\dfrac{10}{n} = \dfrac{12}{30}$

8. $\dfrac{14}{22} = \dfrac{7}{m}$

9. $\dfrac{27}{a} = \dfrac{18}{8}$

10. $\dfrac{90}{45} = \dfrac{100}{x}$

11. $\dfrac{x}{105} = \dfrac{7}{15}$

12. $\dfrac{4}{9} = \dfrac{7}{y}$

13. $\dfrac{a+1}{12} = \dfrac{2}{3}$

14. $\dfrac{2}{6} = \dfrac{n+1}{9}$

15. $\dfrac{12}{9} = \dfrac{y-3}{6}$

Total Problems: ___ Total Correct: ___ Score: ___

Name _____

Study the box below. Write each fraction as a percent. Round to the nearest hundredth. Write the answer in the space provided.

Rule:	Example:
To change a fraction to a percent:	$\dfrac{5}{8}$
1. Change the fraction to a decimal.	
Divide the numerator by the denominator.	$5 \div 8 = .625$
2. Change the decimal to a percent.	
Multiply by 100, which moves the decimal point 2 places to the right. Add a 0 if necessary, and do not forget the percent sign.	**62.5%**

1. $\dfrac{27}{100} =$

2. $\dfrac{7}{8} =$

3. $\dfrac{9}{10} =$

4. $\dfrac{3}{2} =$

5. $\dfrac{8}{16} =$

6. $\dfrac{3}{4} =$

7. $\dfrac{2}{3} =$

8. $\dfrac{5}{3} =$

9. $1\dfrac{5}{8} =$

10. $\dfrac{26}{20} =$

11. $\dfrac{1}{125} =$

12. $2\dfrac{1}{2} =$

Study the box below. Write each percent as a fraction or mixed number in lowest terms in the space provided.

Rule:	Example:
To change a percent to a fraction:	$70\% = \dfrac{70}{100} = \dfrac{7}{10}$
1. Drop the percent sign and place the number over 100.	
2. Reduce to lowest terms.	

13. $35\% =$

14. $5\% =$

15. $74\% =$

16. $1\% =$

17. $91\dfrac{3}{4}\% =$

18. $12\dfrac{1}{2}\% =$

19. $10\dfrac{1}{4}\% =$

20. $3\dfrac{1}{3}\% =$

Total Problems:	Total Correct:	Score:

33

Study the box below. In the space provided, write each decimal as a percent.

> **Examples:**
>
> | | |
> |---|---|
> | 0.72 | 3.09 |
> | 0.72 x 100 = | 3.09 x 100 = |
> | **72%** | **309%** |

1. 0.45 =	**4.** 0.9 =	**7.** 0.576 =	**10.** 3.456 =
2. 0.08 =	**5.** 2.25 =	**8.** 0.004 =	**11.** 5.38 =
3. 0.85 =	**6.** 0.035 =	**9.** 0.608 =	**12.** 0.57 =

Study the box below. In the space provided, write each percent as a decimal.

Rule:	**Examples:**	
To change a percent to a decimal: Divide by 100 (which moves the decimal point 2 places to the left).	31% 31 ÷ 100 = **0.31**	4% 4 ÷ 100 = **0.04**

13. 72% =	**16.** 90% =	**19.** 25% =	**22.** $10\frac{1}{2}\% =$
14. 9% =	**17.** 12.1% =	**20.** $\frac{1}{4}\% =$	**23.** 450% =
15. 17% =	**18.** 200% =	**21.** $\frac{3}{4}\% =$	**24.** 80% =

Total Problems: **Total Correct:**   **Score:**

Name _____

Study the box below. Estimate. Write the answer in the space provided.

Rule:	Examples:	8% of 12
One way to estimate percents is to change the percent to a close fraction and round the number.	40% of 62 $\dfrac{2}{5}$ x 60 = **24**	10% of 12 $\dfrac{1}{10}$ x 12 = **1.2**

1. 51% of 228 =

2. 73% of 200 =

3. 89% of 300 =

4. 1% of 198 =

5. 24% of 21 =

6. 37% of 99 =

7. 33% of 20 =

8. 66% of 240 =

9. 26% of 64 =

10. 74% of 40 =

11. 29% of 61 =

12. 47% of $25.95 =

13. 9% of 310 =

14. 290% of 500 =

15. 0.9% of 350 =

16. 150% of 52 =

17. 19% of 50 =

18. 193% of 700 =

19. 1.2% of 200 =

20. 98% of 250 =

21. 34% of 90 =

Total Problems: **Total Correct:**   **Score:**

Study the box below. Solve and round to the nearest tenth. Write the answer in the space provided.

Rule:

Percent Proportion: $\dfrac{\text{Part}}{\text{Whole}} = \dfrac{\%}{100}$

Identify the part, whole, and/or percent.

Then, plug the numbers into the proportion and solve for the piece that is missing (part, whole, or percent).

Example:

27 is 60% of what number?

$\dfrac{27}{x} = \dfrac{60}{100}$

$60x = 2{,}700$

$x = 45$

27 is 60% of 45.

---

1. 45 is 50% of what number?

2. Find 4% of $2,060.

3. 65 is what percent of 98?

4. 88 is 160% of what number?

5. What number is 6% of $9.40?

6. 25% of 450 is what number?

7. 60 is what percent of 150?

8. What number is 35% of 40?

9. What percent of 24 is 8?

10. Find 70% of 80.

11. What number is 30% of 412?

12. What percent of 70 is 42?

36

Total Problems: _____   **Total Correct:** _____   **Score:** _____

Study the box below. Find the interest and the total amount. Round to the nearest cent. Write the answer in the space provided.

Rule:

Simple Interest Formula: $I = prt$

I = interest
p = principal
r = rate
t = time (expressed in years)

Example:

principal: $600

rate: $6\frac{1}{2}\%$

time: 9 months

I = 600 • 0.0625 • 0.75 = **$28.13**

Total = interest + principal
Total = $28.13 + $600.00 = **$628.13**

1. principal: $95
   rate: 18%
   time: 2 years

5. principal: $695
   rate: 5%
   time: 15 months

2. principal: $400
   rate: 1%
   time: 6 months

6. principal: $425
   rate: 10%
   time: 4 years

3. principal: $2500
   rate: 12%
   time: 3 years

7. principal: $90
   rate: 8%
   time: 21 months

4. principal: $70
   rate: 2%
   time: 3 months

8. principal: $10,000
   rate: 12%
   time: 18 months

Write a proportion for each problem, then solve. Write the answer in the space provided.

1. Bill works 5 hours as a landscaper and earns $53.25. If he works 8 hours, how much does he earn?

5. Dwayne made 17 out of 20 attempted field goals during his second season. What percentage of field goals did he make?

2. Raymond must score a 70% on his history test to pass. If there are 150 questions on the test, how many must he answer correctly?

6. There are 35 students in Mr. Carlyle's class. Ten of the students are male, and the rest are female. What percentage of the students in Mr. Carlyle's class are male? female?

3. On a map with a scale of 2 inches : 75 miles, what would be the distance between cities A and B if they measured 5 inches apart on the map?

7. Of the 18 middle schools in Ms. Hale's district, 13 have more than 60 computers. What percentage of the schools have more than 60 computers?

4. On her science test, Shawna correctly answered 66 out of 78 questions. What percent of the questions did she answer correctly?

8. Janet swims 36 laps in the pool in 45 minutes. At this rate, how many laps will she swim in an hour?

Total Problems: **Total Correct:** **Score:**

Study the box below. In the space provided, write an algebraic expression or equation for each phrase.

Rule:	Example:
Look for key words which indicate addition, subtraction, multiplication, division, or equals.	The product of x and 15 is 60. The word "product" suggests multiplication and "is" means an equal sign. **15x = 60**

1. 3 more than x

2. 8 less than y

3. 12 increased by y

4. 4 minus r

5. A number divided by 5

6. The sum of 7 and e

7. 24 more than a number is 43.

8. The product of m and 6

9. The quotient of 12 and x

10. Seven times a number is 14.

11. A number increased by 5 is 11.

12. A number decreased by 7 is 9.

13. One-third of the sum of x and 5 is 25.

14. Three more than the product of 5 and x is 20.

Name _____

Study the box below. Follow the directions. Write the answer on the line provided.

Rule:	Example:
Replace each variable with the given value and then evaluate.	Evaluate $xy + 5$ if $x = 4$ and $y = 6$. $4 \times 6 + 5 = \mathbf{29}$

Evaluate each expression if $a = 3$, $b = 5$, and $c = 6$.

1. $(c - a) + 8b$ _____

2. $bc \div a$ _____

3. $ac - 10$ _____

4. $a^2 + b^2$ _____

5. $2a - 3b$ _____

6. $(25 \div b)^2$ _____

7. $6c + b^2 - a^2$ _____

8. ab^2 _____

9. $(ab)^2$ _____

Evaluate each expression if $w = 9$, $x = 7$, $y = 10$, and $z = 4$.

10. $\dfrac{xy}{5}$ _____

11. $w^2 - yz$ _____

12. $2yz$ _____

13. $wxy \div 5$ _____

14. $z^2 - 2x$ _____

15. $(wz \div 6)^2$ _____

16. $xy - wz$ _____

17. $2w + 3x - y$ _____

18. $y^2 - wx$ _____

Total Problems: ____ Total Correct: ____ Score: ____

Study the box below. Solve and check each equation in the space provided.

Rules:

Solve each equation by using the inverse operation.

To check the equation, replace the variable with the solution.

Example:

$m - 2.4 = {}^-3.2$

$m - 2.4 + 2.4 = {}^-3.2 + 2.4$

$m = {}^-0.8$

Check: ${}^-0.8 - 2.4 = {}^-3.2$

${}^-3.2 = {}^-3.2$

1. $x + 76 = 89$

2. $m - 27 = 51$

3. $a + 12.4 = 9.2$

4. $r - 41 = 27$

5. $b + 73 = 209$

6. $49 = y - 65$

7. $c + 6.2 = 8.5$

8. $p + 435 = 924$

9. $r - 64 = 157$

10. $x + 152 = 28$

11. ${}^-120 = x + 59$

12. $m - 4.6 = 7.7$

13. $b - 37 = {}^-61$

14. $k + 18.3 = 29.1$

15. $306 = m + 198$

16. $74 = x + 137$

17. $r + 30 = {}^-214$

18. $142 = x - 38$

Total Problems:	Total Correct:	Score:

Study the box below. Solve and check each equation in the space provided.

Rule:	Example:
Solve each equation by using the inverse operation.	$^-36a = 936$ $^-36a \div ^-36 = 936 \div ^-36$ **a = $^-$26**
To check the equation, replace the variable with the solution.	Check: $^-36 \times ^-26 = 936$ $\qquad\qquad 936 = 936$

1. $26y = 910$

2. $475 = 19b$

3. $4.3x = 17.2$

4. $x \div 41 = 5$

5. $^-7.2m = 43.2$

6. $a \div 26 = ^-5$

7. $\dfrac{x}{44} = 15$

8. $\dfrac{z}{32} = 16$

9. $\dfrac{c}{23} = ^-11$

10. $760 = 8n$

11. $^-832 = 26y$

12. $31m = 527$

13. $x \div 78 = 38$

14. $36m = 432$

15. $52.16 = 16y$

16. $\dfrac{y}{32} = 6$

17. $\dfrac{x}{33} = ^-42$

18. $\dfrac{m}{47} = ^-26$

Total Problems:	Total Correct:	Score:

Study the box below. Solve and check each equation in the space provided.

Rule:	Example:
Determine the order in which the operations have been applied to the variable.	$^-3m - 4 = 11$
	$^-3m - 4 + 4 = 11 + 4$
Then, use the inverse operation to undo each operation.	$^-3m = 15$
	$^-3m \div -3 = 15 \div ^-3$
To check, replace the variable with the solution to make sure both sides of the equation are equal.	**m = $^-$5**
	Check: $^-3 \bullet ^-5 - 4 = 11$
	$15 - 4 = 11$
	$11 = 11$

1. $^-9 = 2n + 5$

2. $\dfrac{m - 3}{2} = 7$

3. $17 = ^-2r - 3$

4. $^-4 + 8x = 28$

5. $13 = ^-2p + 5$

6. $\dfrac{c - 6}{4} = 0$

7. $^-x + 6 = 12$

8. $\dfrac{y + 3}{6} = 5$

9. $2 + 5a = ^-53$

10. $\dfrac{x}{^-4} + 6 = ^-5$

11. $\dfrac{y}{12} - 6 = 11$

12. $\dfrac{m - 4}{^-3} = 5$

13. $^-9y - 36 = 36$

14. $^-3x - 15 = 18$

15. $15 + 4r = 31$

Name _____

Study the box below. Solve and check each equation in the space provided.

Example:

$$m - \frac{1}{2} = \frac{-3}{8}$$

$$m - \frac{1}{2} + \frac{1}{2} = \frac{3}{8} + \frac{1}{2}$$

$$m = \frac{1}{8}$$

Check: $\frac{1}{8} - \frac{1}{2} = \frac{-3}{8}$

$$-\frac{1}{8} = \frac{4}{8} \quad \frac{-3}{8}$$

$$\frac{-3}{8} = \frac{-3}{8}$$

1. $-6n = \frac{11}{12}$

2. $\frac{2}{3}x = -1\frac{4}{5}$

3. $\frac{y}{4} = \frac{-2}{9}$

4. $\frac{-3}{5} + x = 1$

5. $p - \frac{7}{8} = 1\frac{1}{3}$

6. $\frac{m}{-3} = \frac{11}{15}$

7. $-6 = \frac{11}{12}b$

8. $2\frac{1}{2} = -5y$

9. $2\frac{1}{6}y = 6\frac{1}{2}$

10. $\frac{3}{4} = x - 1\frac{1}{2}$

11. $-9 = \frac{2}{3}y$

12. $\frac{1}{2} = r - 1\frac{4}{5}$

Total Problems: _____ Total Correct: _____ Score: _____

Name _____

Study the box below. Solve and check each equation in the space provided.

Rule:	Example:
1. Combine all like terms that have the same variable by adding or subtracting.	$54 = 3y + 6y$ $54 = 9y$ **$y = 6$**
2. Solve the equation for the variable.	
3. Check the equation by replacing each variable with the solution.	Check: $54 = 3 \cdot 6 + 6 \cdot 6$ $54 = 18 + 36$ $54 = 54$

1. $^-121 = 3x + 8x$

2. $19v - 7v = ^-108$

3. $4b + 5b = 81$

4. $7x + x = 32$

5. $24x - 18x = 36$

6. $^-65 = 13a - 8a$

7. $12m - 2m = 90$

8. $60 = 16y - y$

9. $7x - 4x = ^-45$

10. $6a + 12a = 108$

11. $^-35 = ^-8x + 9x$

12. $9y - 2y = ^-63$

13. $28y - 14y = ^-42$

14. $8c + 9c = 51$

15. $^-3a + 10a = 49$

16. $3.4m + 4.6m = 72$

17. $348 = 47h - 18h$

18. $43 = 6.2x + 2.4x$

Total Problems: **Total Correct:** **Score:**

Study the box below. Solve and check each equation in the space provided.

Rule:	Example:
Simplify all expressions in the equation by using the following properties: **Commutative:** the order of elements produces no change in the result. **Associative:** grouping two elements differently produces no change in the result. **Distributive:** when a number is multiplied by a group of numbers, that number can be distributed to each number in the group. Then, solve the equation and check the solution.	$2(6n) + 12 + 4n = 60$ $12n + 12 + 4n = 60$ $16n + 12 = 60$ $16n = 48$ **$n = 3$** Check: $2(6 \cdot 3) + 12 + 4 \cdot 3 = 60$ $36 + 12 + 12 = 60$ **$60 = 60$**

1. $62 = 9y + 5(y+4)$

5. $^-b + 5 + 11b = {}^-55$

9. $4(c + 5) + 11c = 110$

2. $3(m - 1) + 4m = {}^-73$

6. $4(m + 3) - 7m = 54$

10. $8y + 9(y + 6) = 105$

3. $2(x + 9) + 3 = 45$

7. $20 = 14n - 9 + 3(5n)$

11. $^-2(x + 3) + 6(^-x) = 34$

4. $8c + 5(c - 6) = 9$

8. $^-3(6x) - 8 + 4x = 76$

12. $6(y - 4) + 2y + 8y = 72$

Total Problems: _____   Total Correct: _____   Score: _____

Study the box below. Solve and check each equation in the space provided.

Rule:

When there are variables on both sides of the equation, move all of the variables to one side of equation and the numbers to the other side.

Then, solve the equation for the variable and check the solution.

Example:

$6x = 24 + 2x$
$6x - 2x = 24 + 2x - 2x$
$4x = 24$
$x = 6$

Check: $6 \cdot 6 = 24 + 2 \cdot 6$
$\qquad\quad 36 = 36$

---

1. $4y + 9 = 3y$

2. $8m = 5m + 18$

3. $16h = 72 + 7h$

4. $^-4r + 15 = r$

5. $108 - 7x = {^-}4x$

6. $63 + 9y = 16y$

7. $18b = 63 - 3b$

8. $3p + 9 = {^-}15p$

9. $14f + 4 = 9f - 11$

10. $9m + 27 = 6m$

11. $4(x - 2) = 6x - 10$

12. $4(a + 2) = 2(a + 6)$

13. $\dfrac{1}{2}(x + 18) = 19$

14. $\dfrac{5}{6}y = \dfrac{1}{3}(y + 6)$

15. $\dfrac{5}{7}n + 12 = \dfrac{3}{7}n + 4$

Total Problems:	Total Correct:	Score:

47

Name _____

Study the box below. Solve each inequality. Write the answer in the space provided.

Rule:	Examples:	
Solve an inequality the same way you would solve an equation. However, when multiplying or dividing by a negative number, reverse the sign of the inequality.	$y + 4 \geq {}^-9$ $y + 4 - 4 \geq {}^-9 - 4$ **$y \geq {}^-13$** Any number greater than or equal to $^-13$ is a solution.	$^-2y < 10$ $^-2y \div {}^-2 < 10 \div {}^-2$ **$y > {}^-5$** Any number greater than $^-5$ is a solution.

1. $108 \geq {}^-9b$

2. $^-8 + a > 10$

3. $^-30 \leq x + ({}^-5)$

4. $\dfrac{x}{3} > {}^-15$

5. $\dfrac{c}{7} < 12$

6. $12 > \dfrac{n}{5}$

7. $3y < {}^-48$

8. $^-27 < {}^-3m$

9. $12 + x > {}^-9$

10. $p + 13 > {}^-13$

11. $^-15 - y < 0$

12. $^-6r \geq 72$

13. $7f + 3 > 52$

14. $4x - 7 \geq {}^-35$

15. $2(x + 3) > 12$

16. $\dfrac{r}{^-2} - 5 > 27$

17. $\dfrac{m}{5} + 12 \geq 32$

18. $37 \leq \dfrac{a}{2} + 12$

Total Problems:	Total Correct:	Score:

Study the box below. Solve each inequality in the space provided.

Rule:	Example:
Solve inequalities with combined operations in the same way that you would solve an equation. Remember to reverse the sign of the inequality when multiplying or dividing by a negative number.	$^-16 + 3a > {}^-5a$ $^-16 > {}^-8a$ **$2 < a$** **$a > 2$** Any number greater than 2 is a solution.

1. $10 - 2y \le {}^-2$

2. $^-2 \ge {}^-3x - 4$

3. $2h + 1 < 13$

4. $48 > {}^-7m + 6$

5. $4c - 7 > 21$

6. $21 - 4x \le 29$

7. $\dfrac{a}{^-20} > {}^-3.7$

8. $\dfrac{c}{5} + 26 \ge 51$

9. $\dfrac{a}{^-2} - 9 \le 11$

10. $^-21 \ge 3\,(b + 5)$

11. $^-2\,(n - 4) \le 10$

12. $3 - 9x \le 30$

13. $13 \ge 3y - 5$

14. $7 + 8y > 39$

15. $4 \le 2\,(x - 6)$

16. $10y - 5 > 4y - 3$

17. $^-12m + 40 \le 9m - 2$

18. $5c - 21 < 11c + 9$

Total Problems:	Total Correct:	Score:

49

Solve each problem. Show your work and write the answers in the space provided.

1. Solve for **a** in the equation $a + b = c$.

2. If **a** represents Alexander's age and **c** represents Carlton's age, explain what is meant by $a = c + 5$.

3. Harriett's 4-person relay team won the race in 46 seconds. What was the average time for each person?

4. Sydney's softball team won 18 games during her senior year. They won 9 more games than they lost. How many games did they lose?

5. The corner bakery charges $5.00 for a dozen bagels. How much does each bagel cost?

6. A large soda at the theater costs $0.50 more than a small. A small soda costs $1.75. How much do 2 small sodas and 3 large sodas cost?

7. Sylvan earns $35 a day at his job, plus $4 per hour of overtime. If he made $55 for one day's work, how many hours of overtime did he work?

8. Solve the following equations for y.

   A. $y + y = y$

   B. $5 + y = y + 5$

Total Problems: _____   Total Correct: _____   Score: _____

Study the box below. Simplify. Write the answer in the space provided.

Rule:	Example:
A **monomial** is the product of any number of factors. A **polynomial** is a monomial or the sum or difference of monomials. To simplify polynomials, combine all like terms.	$3m^3 - 5 - 6m^3 + 10$ $^-3m^3 + 5$

1. $3y - 7y$

2. $x - 8x$

3. $4x^3 + 5x^3 - 7$

4. $^-2x^5 - 5x^5 + 6$

5. $7y^4 - 2y^4 - 2$

6. $3x^2 - x + 4x^2 + 6x$

7. $5b^4 - 3b + 3b + b^4$

8. $6y^2 - y - y^2 + 8$

9. $2m - 3m^3 + 16 - 2m^3$

Evaluate each polynomial if a = $^-5$, b = $^-2$, c = 3, and d = $^-4$.

10. $b^3 + 15$

11. $a^2 + a$

12. $c^3 + 2c^2$

13. $^-5a - 2d$

14. $d^2 + 3b^2$

15. ^-abc

16. $3ab - d^2$

17. $a^2 - c^2 + b^3$

18. $3b + 5ad$

Name _____

Study the box below. Add. Write the answer in the space provided.

Rule:	Example:
To add polynomials, add their like terms.	$(4y + 2) + (^-3y - 1)$
One way to do this is to rewrite the like terms in columns.	$\begin{array}{r} 4y + 2 \\ + \quad ^-3y - 1 \\ \hline \mathbf{y + 1} \end{array}$

1. $(6x^2 + 5x) + (^-7x^2 - 3x)$

2. $(5y^3 + 2y^2) + (2y^3 - y^2)$

3. $(4y^4 - 3y^3) + (y^4 + 2y^3)$

4. $(b^2 + 12) + (2b^2 - 7)$

5. $\begin{array}{r} ^-5x^2 + 3x - 7 \\ + \quad x^2 + 2x + 5 \\ \hline \end{array}$

6. $(8ab^2 + 9b) + (3a^2b + 4b)$

7. $(6c^3 + 10) + (^-4c^3 - 10)$

8. $(8y^2 + y) + (^-6y^2 - 2y + 3)$

9. $(6a^3 - a^2) + (4a^2 + 5)$

10. $\begin{array}{r} 5x^2 - x + 6 \\ + \quad 3x^2 + 4x - 7 \\ \hline \end{array}$

Total Problems: _____ Total Correct: _____ Score: _____

Study the box below. Subtract. Write the answer in the space provided.

Rule:	Example:
To subtract polynomials, add their additive inverse. It may be helpful to write the like terms in columns.	$(5x + 6) - (4x - 8)$ $5x + 6 + (^-4x + 8)$ $\quad 5x + 6$ $+ \; ^-4x + 8$ ——————— $\quad\quad x + 14$

1. $(6m + 5) - (m + 3)$

2. $(^-3a - 5) - (5a + 4)$

3. $(2x^2 + 2) - (3x^2 + 4)$

4. $(8b - 5) - (b + 9)$

5. $(4y^2 + 3y + 2) - (^-y^2 - 4y)$

6. $(5 + 6y) - (3 - 2y)$

7. $(a^3 - 3a^2) - (4a^3 + 2a^2)$

8. $(3y^2 - 5y - 2) - (3y^2 + 6y - 8)$

9. $(5a + 6) - (^-6a + 8)$

10. $(3m^2 + 3m - 2) - (^-2m^2 + 2m - 5)$

Study the box below. Find each product. Write the answer in the space provided.

Rule:	Example:
Use the distributive property to multiply a monomial by a polynomial.	$2y(3y + 4)$ $2y \cdot 3y + 2y \cdot 4$ **$6y^2 + 8y$**

1. $4x(2x + 5)$

2. $a(2a - 4)$

3. $2y\ (^-y + 4)$

4. $6b^2(^-3b + 2)$

5. $^-5x(^-3x^4 - 2x)$

6. $2y^3(y^3 + 4)$

7. $2x^2(3x^4 + 4x^3)$

8. $3a(^-3a^4b + a^2)$

9. $10y(^-y^4 - 2xy^2)$

Study the box below. Find each product. Write the answer in the space provided.

Rule:	Example:
When multiplying two binomials, use the distributive property twice.	$(y + 2)(y^2 + 3)$ $y(y^2 + 3) + 2(y^2 + 3)$ $y^3 + 3y + 2y^2 + 6$ **$y^3 + 2y^2 + 3y + 6$**

10. $(a^2 - 4)(a - 5)$

11. $(b^3 + 2)(b + 1)$

12. $(c^4 - 2)(c + 4)$

13. $(2x + 2)(2x + 3)$

14. $(y - 6)(y + 6)$

15. $(xy + 3x^2)(xy - 3x^2)$

Total Problems:	Total Correct:	Score:

Name _____

Study the box below. Find each quotient. Write the answer in the space provided.

Rule:	Example:
Divide by factoring the numerator and denominator, then cancel.	$\dfrac{6a^3}{3a}$ $\dfrac{2 \cdot \cancel{3} \cdot \cancel{a} \cdot a \cdot a}{\cancel{3} \cdot \cancel{a}}$
	$2a^2$

1. $\dfrac{3b^2}{15b}$

3. $\dfrac{35b^5}{5b^3}$

5. $\dfrac{21a^4}{3a}$

2. $\dfrac{16y^4}{4y^2}$

4. $\dfrac{9y^5}{9y^3}$

6. $\dfrac{34x}{17}$

Study the box below. Find each quotient. Write the answer in the space provided.

Rule:	Example:
To divide a polynomial by a monomial, divide each term of the polynomial by the monomial, then simplify.	$(4b^2 - 8b + 12) \div 4$ $4b^2 \div 4 - 8b \div 4 + 12 \div 4$ **$b^2 - 2b + 3$**

7. $(24x^2 - 8x + 16) \div 8$

9. $(5x^3 - 7x^2 + x) \div x$

11. $(18x^5 + 27x^4 + 9x^3) \div 9x^3$

8. $(12a^2 - 6a + 6) \div 6$

10. $(14c^3 - 21c^2 + 7c) \div 7c$

12. $(x^4 - 4x^3 + x^2) \div x^2$

Total Problems:	Total Correct:	Score:

55

To identify the coordinates of each point, use the coordinate system. Write in which of the quadrants each point lies.

1. A

2. B

3. C

4. D

5. E

6. F

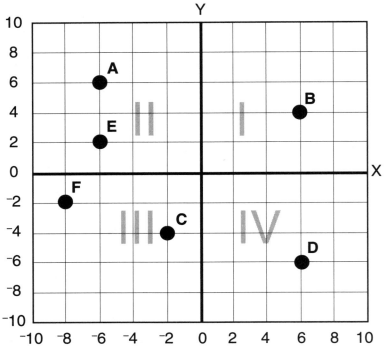

On graph paper, draw a coordinate plane. Then, graph and label each point.

7. G (-3, 2)

8. H (-5, 0)

9. I (2, 4)

10. J (0, 4)

11. K (7, 7)

12. L (0, 0)

13. M (-6, -4)

14. N (-9, 1)

Total Problems: _____   Total Correct: _____   Score: _____

Study the box below. Solve and graph the solutions on a number line in the space
provided.

Rule:	**Example:**
Solve the inequality.	$3y - 4 < 2$
To graph the solution on a number line, shade the part of the number line indicated by the solution. A hollow circle indicates the solution is not included. A solid circle indicates the solution is included.	$3y - 4 + 4 < 2 + 4$ $3y < 6$ $3y \div 3 < 6 \div 3$ **$y < 2$** 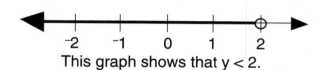 This graph shows that $y < 2$.

1. $n - 1 > {}^-6$

2. $^-2h \leq 6$

3. $c + 8 \geq {}^-2$

4. $7m - 8 \leq 20$

5. $3p - 9 > {}^-24$

6. $2r - 10 \geq 4$

7. $5y - 3 \geq 12$

8. $^-2d + 1 < 5$

9. $^-3m + 6 \leq {}^-3$

10. $^-2a + 4 \geq 6$

Name _____

Study the box below. In the space provided, make a table of solutions for each equation. Use values of ⁻1, 0, 1, and 3 for x. Write the solution as ordered pairs.

Rule:

The table should have 3 columns.

Substitute each value of x for the expression in the middle of the table.

Do the computation to find y.

Example:

$y = 2x + 1$

x	2x + 1	y
⁻1	2 (⁻1) + 1	⁻1
0	2 (0) +1	1
1	2 (1) + 1	3
3	2 (3) + 1	7

The ordered pairs are as follows:
(⁻1, ⁻1); (0, 1); (1, 3); (3, 7)

1. $y = x + 3$

4. $y = ⁻3x + 5$

2. $y = 4x$

5. $y = ⁻3x - 1$

3. $y = 2x - 3$

6. $y = 5x - 8$

Total Problems: **Total Correct:**   **Score:**

Study the box below. Make a table of solutions and list the ordered pairs. Then, graph each equation.

Example:

$y = 2x + 2$

Table of Solutions

x	2x + 2	y
⁻1	2 (⁻1) + 2	0
0	2 (0) + 2	2
1	2 (1) + 2	4
3	2 (3) + 2	8

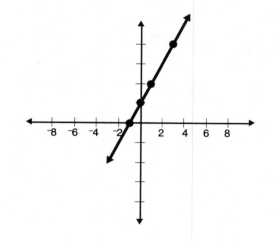

ordered pairs: (⁻1, 0); (0, 2); (1, 4); (3, 8)

1. $y = x - 3$

2. $y = ⁻6x + 1$

3. $y = ⁻2x + 2$

Name _____

Study the box below. Find the slope of each line given two points on the line.

+---+
Rule:	**Example:**
Slope is the steepness of a	(⁻4, ⁻2); (5, 3)
line.	
	Change in y: 3 – (⁻2) = 5
To find the slope, compute the	
change in y over the change in x.	Change in x: 5 – (⁻4) = 9
	The slope is $\frac{5}{9}$.
+---+

1. (⁻4, ⁻1); (⁻2, 3)

6. (⁻4, 3); (3, 4)

11. (7, 3); (⁻1, ⁻3)

2. (⁻2, 5); (1, 6)

7. (3, 4); (⁻2, 3)

12. (⁻3, 3); (3, ⁻3)

3. (5, 10); (⁻2, ⁻3)

8. (⁻2, ⁻3); (1, ⁻5)

13. (⁻3, 7); (4, ⁻6)

4. (3, 2); (⁻1, ⁻4)

9. (6, ⁻3); (5, ⁻3)

14. (⁻5, ⁻7); (⁻1, 3)

5. (6, 4); (⁻2, 2)

10. (2, 4); (5, 8)

15. (⁻3, ⁻2); (3, 5)

60

Total Problems: **Total Correct:**   **Score:**

Name _____

Study the box below. Find the x- and y-intercepts of each line. Write the answer in the space provided.

Rules:	Example:
The **x-intercept** is the point at which the line crosses the x-axis. To find the x-intercept, find the value of x when y=0.	$y = 2x + 3$
	x-intercept
	$0 = 2x + 3$
The **y-intercept** is the point at which the line crosses the y-axis. To find the y-intercept, find the value of y when x=0.	$2x = {}^-3$
	$x = \dfrac{{}^-3}{2}$

Example y-intercept:
$y = 2(0) + 3$
$y = \mathbf{3}$

1. $y = x - 2$

3. $y = {}^-x - 3$

5. $y = 4x - 3$

2. $y = x + 6$

4. $y = 3x + 2$

6. $y = {}^-3x + 5$

Study the box below. Find the x- and y-intercepts and their ordered pairs. On a separate sheet of paper, graph each line.

Rule:	Example:
To graph a line, graph both ordered pairs and "connect the dots," drawing the line that contains both points.	line: $y = 2x + 3$
	x-intercept: $\dfrac{{}^-3}{2}$ ordered pair: $(\dfrac{{}^-3}{2}, 0)$
	y-intercept: **3** ordered pair: **(0, 3)**

7. $y = x + 3$

8. $y = 2x - 5$

9. $y = 4x + 2$

Total Problems:	Total Correct:	Score:

Study the box below. Each pair of angles is either complementary or supplementary. In the space provided, find the degree measure for each angle.

Rule:

If the sum of 2 angles equals 90°, the angles are **complementary**.

If the sum of 2 angles equals 180°, the angles are **supplementary**.

Example:

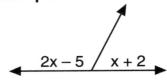

$2x - 5 + x + 2 = 180$
$3x - 3 = 180$
$3x = 183$
$x = 61°$

1.

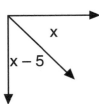

x

$x - 5$

3.

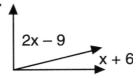

$2x - 9$

$x + 6$

5.

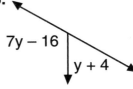

$7y - 16$

$y + 4$

2.

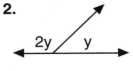

$2y$ y

4.

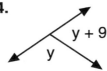

$y + 9$

y

6.

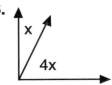

x

$4x$

Study the example below. In the space provided, write and solve an equation to find the following.

Example:

Find the supplement of a 78° angle.

$x + 78 = 180$
$x + 78 - 78 = 180 - 78$
$x = 102°$

7. Find the complement of an 18° angle.

9. Find the supplement of a 53° angle.

8. Find the supplement of a 147° angle

10. Find the complement of a 27° angle.

Total Problems: **Total Correct:**   **Score:**

Study the rules below. Classify each triangle by its sides and angles. Write the answers in the space provided.

Rules: By sides:	**Equilateral** 3 equal sides	**Isosceles** 2 equal sides	**Scalene** 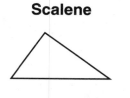 no equal sides
By angles:	**Acute** 3 acute angles	**Obtuse** 1 obtuse angle	**Right** 1 right angle

1.

5m   5m
5m

2.

3.

2km   2km

Study the box below. Find the value of x in each triangle. Write the answer in the space provided.

Rule: The sum of the measures of the angles of any triangle is 180°.	**Example:** 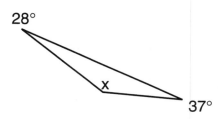

4.
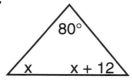
80°
x   x + 12

5.

28°
x
37°

Name _____

Study the rules below. Classify each quadrilateral as a square, rectangle, rhombus, parallelogram, or trapezoid. (Some quadrilaterals may have more than one name.) Then, circle which name best describes the figure.

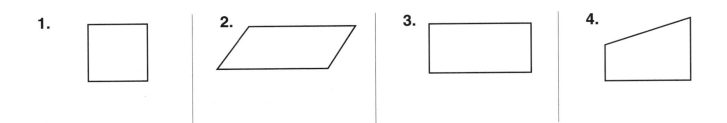

Rules:	Square	Parallelogram	Rectangle	Rhombus	Trapezoid
	All sides equal All angles 90°	Opposite sides parallel	Opposite sides equal All angles 90°	All sides equal Opposite angles equal	1 pair of parallel sides

1.   2.   3.   4.

Study the box below. Find the value of x in each quadrilateral. Write the answer in the space provided.

> **Rule:**
>
> The sum of the measures of the angles of any quadrilateral is 360°.

5.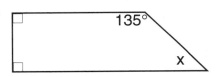

7.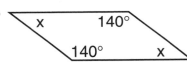

6.

8.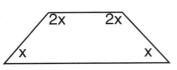

Total Problems:	Total Correct:	Score:

Name _____

Study the box below. Use the Pythagorean Theorem to find the length of the hypotenuse of each right triangle. The lengths of the legs are given. Round answers to the nearest tenth and write the answer on the line provided.

Rule:	Example:
The Pythagorean Theorem states: In a right triangle, the square of the measure of the hypotenuse is equal to the sum of the squares of the lengths of the legs. $a^2 + b^2 = c^2$ 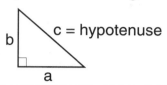	6 m , 8 m $6^2 + 8^2 = c^2$ $36 + 64 = c^2$ $100 = c^2$ $\sqrt{100} = c$ **c = 10 m**

1. 24 in, 7 in _____

2. 5 m, 18 m _____

3. 15 cm, 36 cm _____

4. 15 in, 20 in _____

5. 6 km, 6 km _____

6. 12 cm, 9 cm _____

7. 16 m, 30 m _____

8. 12 m, 20 m _____

9. 6 ft, 10 ft _____

Given the following lengths, determine whether each triangle is a right triangle. Write "yes" or "no" on the line provided.

10. 5 m, 12 m, 13m _____

11. 11 m, 60 m, 61 m _____

12. 4 ft, 5 ft, 8 ft _____

13. 7 in, 15 in, 21 in _____

14. 9 m, 11 m, 17 m _____

15. 9 cm, 29 cm, 36 cm _____

Study the box below. Find the perimeter of each figure. Write the answer in the space provided.

Rule:

Perimeter is the distance around a figure.

To find the perimeter, find the sum of all of the sides.

Example:

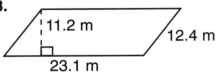

4.1m

11.9 m

P = 2(4.1 + 11.9)
P = **32m**

1.

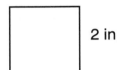

2 in

3.

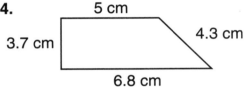

11.2 m   12.4 m

23.1 m

2.

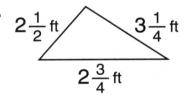

$2\frac{1}{2}$ ft $3\frac{1}{4}$ ft

$2\frac{3}{4}$ ft

4.

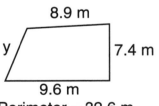

5 cm

4.3 cm

3.7 cm

6.8 cm

Use the perimeter of each figure to find the value of x.

5.

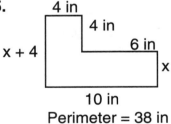

4 in

4 in

6 in

x + 4

x

10 in

Perimeter = 38 in

6.

8.9 m

y   7.4 m

9.6 m

Perimeter = 32.6 m

Total Problems: **Total Correct:**   **Score:**

Name _____

Study the box below. Find the area of each figure. Write the answer in the space provided.

Rule:	Examples:	
Area is the measure of the space inside a shape. Rectangle: A = length x width Parallelogram: A = base x height	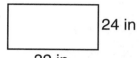 32 in A = l x w 32 x 24 = **768 in²**	4 m / 5 m 22 m A = b x h 22 x 4 = **88m²**

1.

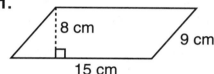

8 cm

9 cm

15 cm

4.   Rectangle

length = 21.5 m

width = 12.6 m

2.

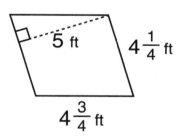

5 ft

$4\frac{1}{4}$ ft

$4\frac{3}{4}$ ft

5.   Rectangle

length = 30 in

width = 6 in

3.

5.7 m   12.2 m

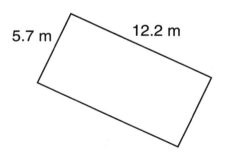

6.   Parallelogram

base = $3\frac{1}{2}$ ft

height = $2\frac{1}{4}$ ft

Name _____

Study the box below. Find the area of each triangle. Round to the nearest hundredth. Write the answer in the space provided.

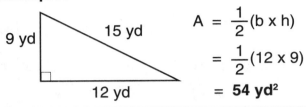

Rule:	**Example:**
The area of a triangle = $\frac{1}{2}$(b x h), where b is the base and h is the height.	$A = \frac{1}{2}$(b x h) $= \frac{1}{2}$(12 x 9) = **54 yd²**

1.

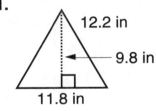

12.2 in
9.8 in
11.8 in

2.

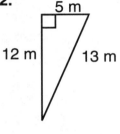

5 m
12 m
13 m

3.

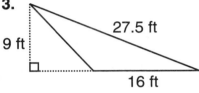

27.5 ft
9 ft
16 ft

Study the box below. Find the area of each trapezoid. Round to the nearest hundredth. Write the answer in the space provided.

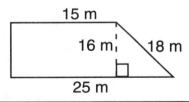

Rule:	**Example:**
The area of trapezoid = $\frac{1}{2}$ h(a + b), where h is the height and a and b are the bases.	$A = \frac{1}{2}$h(a + b) $= \frac{1}{2}$ (16)(15 + 25) = **320 m²**

4.

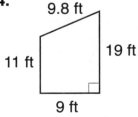

9.8 ft
19 ft
11 ft
9 ft

5. bases: = 0.5 m, 0.3 m

height: = 0.2 m

Total Problems: **Total Correct:**   **Score:**

Name _____

Study the box below. Find the circumference and area of each circle. Use 3.14 for π. Round answers to the nearest hundredth. Write the answers on the lines provided.

Rules:

The circumference is the distance around a circle.
C = πd, where d is the diameter.

The area measures the space inside.
A = πr², where r is the radius.

Remember: d = 2r.

Examples:

$C = \pi d$
$\quad = 3.14 \cdot 4.2$
$\quad = 13.19$ in

$A = \pi r^2$
$\quad = 3.14 \cdot 2.1^2$
$\quad = 13.85$ in²

1.

C = _____
A = _____

5.

9 m

C = _____
A = _____

2.

C = _____
A = _____

6.

$2\frac{1}{2}$ yd

C = _____
A = _____

3.

C = _____
A = _____

7. diameter = 10.6 m

C = _____
A = _____

4.

C = _____
A = _____

8. radius = 0.7 in

C = _____
A = _____

Total Problems: **Total Correct:**   **Score:**   69

Study the box below. Find the volume of each prism or cylinder shown below. Use 3.14 for π. Write the answer in the space provided.

Rules:

Volume is the amount of space occupied by a 3-dimensional object as measured in cubic units.

The volume of a prism = (the area of the base)(height).

The volume of a cylinder = (πr^2)(height).

Remember: In a triangular prism, the triangular face is the base.

Examples:

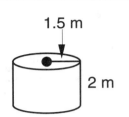

V = Bh
= (5 x 3.5)(4)
= **70 ft³**

$V = \pi r^2 h$
= (3.14)(1.5²)(2)
= **14.13 m³**

1.
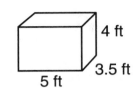
6 yd
10 yd

4.
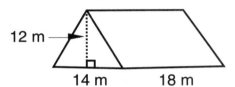
12 m
14 m   18 m

2.
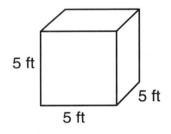
5 ft
5 ft
5 ft

5.
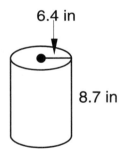
6.4 in
8.7 in

3. Rectangular prism

length = $10\frac{1}{4}$ ft

width = $7\frac{1}{2}$ ft

height = 15 ft

6. Triangular prism

base of triangle: 4m

height of triangle: 4m

height of prism: 4m

Total Problems: ___   **Total Correct:** ___   **Score:** ___

Name _____

Study the box below. Find the volume of each pyramid or cone. Round answers to the nearest tenth. Use 3.14 for π. Write the answer in the space provided.

Rules:

The volume of a pyramid = $\frac{1}{3}$(area of base)(height).

The volume of a cone = $\frac{1}{3}\pi r^2$(height).

Examples:

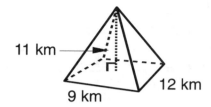

11 km
9 km
12 km

$V = \frac{1}{3}Bh$

$= \frac{1}{3}(9 \cdot 12)(11)$

$= 396 \text{ km}^3$

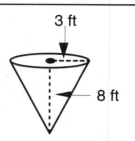

3 ft
8 ft

$V = \frac{1}{3}\pi r^2 h$

$= \frac{1}{3}(3.14)(3^2)(8)$

$= 75.4 \text{ ft}^3$

1.

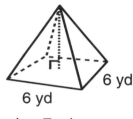

6 yd
6 yd
h = 7 yd

4.

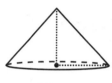

r = 12 m
h = 11 m

2.

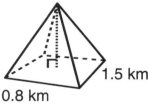

1.5 km
0.8 km
h = 1.8 km

5.

d = 9.8 ft
h = 14 ft

---

3. Rectangular Pyramid

length = 8 in

width = 6 in

height = 17 in

6. Cone

diameter = 10.8 mm

height = 8 mm

Name _____

Study the box below. Find the surface area of each prism or cylinder. Round to nearest tenth. Write the answer in the space provided.

Rule:	**Example:**
The **surface area** of a 3-dimensional figure is the sum of all the areas of its surface.	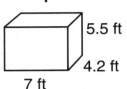 5.5 ft, 4.2 ft, 7 ft 2(5.5 • 4.2) +2(5.5 • 7) + 2(7 • 4.2) = 46.2 + 77 + 58.8 = **182 ft²**

1.

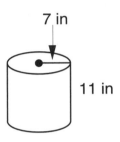

7 in

11 in

Hint: The surface area of a cylinder = 2πr(r +h).

4.

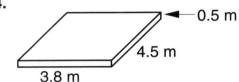

0.5 m

4.5 m

3.8 m

2.

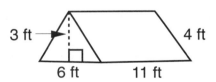

3 ft   4 ft

6 ft   11 ft

5.

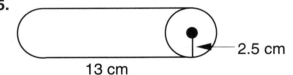

13 cm   2.5 cm

3. Rectangular Prism

length = 6 in

width = $2\frac{1}{2}$ in

height = 5 in

6. Cylinder
radius = 20 mm
height = 13 mm

Total Problems: **Total Correct:**   **Score:**

Solve each problem. Show your work and write the answers in the space provided.

---

1. Find the measure of the complement and supplement of a 23° angle.

4. A circle's circumference and area have the same measure. Find the radius.

---

2. One angle of a triangle measures 32° and another angle measures 66°. What is the measure of the third angle? Classify this triangle by its angles.

5. Austin's rectangular bedroom is 13.5 feet long, 8 feet high, and 10.5 feet wide. He is planning on wallpapering the room. How much wallpaper is needed to cover the walls, not taking into account any doorways or windows?

---

3. One angle of a rhombus measures 45°. What are the measures of the other three angles?

6. A rectangular fish tank is 2.5 feet long by 1.5 feet wide by 1 foot high. If the tank is filled to a height of 10 inches, what is the volume of the water in the tank?

---

7. Fill in each blank with "always," "sometimes," or "never."

A. A rhombus is _____ a square.

B. A trapezoid is _____ a parallelogram.

C. A square is _____ a rhombus.

Study the box below. Use the Fundamental Counting Principle to find the total number of outcomes. Write the answer in the space provided.

Rule:	Example:
To use the **Fundamental Counting Principle**, multiply the number of choices in each set to derive the number of combinations.	Frances needs to buy a new pair of glasses. She can choose from 3 different colors for the frame and 3 tints for the glass. How many different kinds of glasses could Frances select? 3 frames x 3 tints = **9 choices**

1. Rolling 4 dice

4. Tossing 2 quarters and 2 dimes

2. Choosing from 3 shirt colors and 4 sweater vests

5. Choosing an outfit to wear from 4 tops and 5 pairs of pants

3. A quiz has 10 true-false questions. How many different outcomes are possible for giving answers to the 10 questions?

6. Choosing from 3 different kinds of lunch meat, 2 different types of bread, and 3 different kinds of cheese

Total Problems: **Total Correct:**   **Score:**

Name _____

Study the box below. Find the number of permutations. Write the answer in the space provided.

Rule:	**Example:**
A **permutation** is an arrangement of items in a particular order. Solve permutations using factorials (!). A **factorial** is the product of all the positive integers from 1 to n.	Find the number of permutations for the letters A, B, C, and D. How many different ways can A, B, C, and D be arranged? 4 ! = 4 x 3 x 2 x 1 = **24**

1. Tom, Dick, Harry

3. c, o, m, p, u, t, e, r

2. north, south, east, west

4. 0, 1, 2, 3, 4, 5, 6, 7, 8, 9

Study the box below. Find the number of combinations. Write the answer in the space provided.

Rule:	**Example:**
A **combination** is an arrangement of items in which order is not important.	4 new outfits from 10 outfits $\dfrac{10 \cdot 9 \cdot 8 \cdot 7}{4!} = \dfrac{10 \cdot 9 \cdot 8 \cdot 7}{4 \cdot 3 \cdot 2 \cdot 1} = 210$ **There are 210 combinations of outfits.**

5. Three outfielders from 13 players

7. Two volunteers from a group of 10 people

6. Three pizza toppings from 6 choices

8. A 4-person committee from 24 people

Total Problems:	Total Correct:	Score:

Study the box below. Find each probability. Write the answers in the space provided.

Rule:	**Example:**
When one choice does not affect another choice, the outcomes of the events are considered **independent events**. To find the probability of independent events, find the product of both probabilities.	Two dice are rolled. Find the probability of rolling an even number on one die and rolling a 5 on the other. P (even number and 5) = $\frac{1}{2} \cdot \frac{1}{6} = \frac{1}{12}$

1. A die is rolled, then a coin is tossed.

   A. P (odd number and heads)

   B. P (prime number and tails)

   C. P (3 or 4 and heads)

   D. P (3 and tails)

   E. P (number less than 5 and heads)

   F. P (1 and tails)

---

2. A bag contains 3 white marbles, 4 blue ones, 6 green ones, and 5 red ones. One marble is drawn and replaced. Then, a second marble is drawn and replaced.

   A. P (blue and green)

   B. P (green and green)

   C. P (red and white)

   D. P (not a red and white)

---

3. Two dice are rolled.

   A. P (5 and 6)

   B. P (4 and a number less than 3)

   C. P (an even number and 2)

   D. P (2 and a number greater than 3)

Total Problems:	**Total Correct:**	**Score:**

Study the box below. Find each probability. Write the answers in the space provided.

Rule:

When one choice affects another choice, the outcomes of the events are considered **dependent events**. To find the probability of dependent events, find the probability of the first event and multiply it by the probability of the second event.

Example:

Stuart had 5 white socks and 8 blue ones in his drawer. He picks one sock out of the drawer at random and then a second one. What is the probability he will pick a pair of blue socks?

P (blue socks) =
$$\frac{8}{13} \cdot \frac{7}{12} = \frac{14}{39}$$

1.   Kevin has a bag of marbles. There are 3 black, 5 red, 4 blue, 6 green, and 2 white marbles in the bag. Once a marble is drawn, it is not replaced. Find the probability of each event.

   A. P (a white marble and blue one)

   B. P (a green marble and red one)

   C. P (2 black marbles in a row)

   D. P (a red, then blue, then white marble)

   E. P (a white marble 3 times in a row)

   F. P (a blue marble 3 times in a row)

2.   Joe has created a deck of cards. There are 40 cards in the set. Every card has a number between 1 and 10 on it, and every number comes in 4 different colors (red, blue, green, yellow). Once a card is chosen, it is not replaced. Find the probability of each event.

   A. P (a 2 then 3)

   B. P (a blue 3 then 5)

   C. P (a red then yellow)

   D. P (a red 5 and 10)

Study the box below. In the space provided, construct a stem & leaf plot for each set of data.

Rule:	Example:
A stem and leaf plot is a way of displaying data. The digits to the left of the line have the greater place value and are called stems. The digits to the right of the line represent digits in the ones place and are called leaves.	215, 208, 217, 223, 205, 212, 215, 224

stem	leaf
20	58
21	2557
22	34

1. 32, 29, 45, 26, 21, 25, 38, 29, 19, 15, 25

3. 36, 42, 22, 33, 44, 48, 29, 34, 30, 49

2. 325, 343, 356, 339, 340, 327

4. 150, 158, 145, 136, 152, 150, 158, 145

The stem and leaf plot to the right shows final averages for the students in Ms. Collins's English class. Use the stem and leaf plot to answer the following questions.

stem	leaf
6	278
7	055889
8	12357789
9	0159

5. What is the lowest average? highest? _____

6. How many students are in Ms. Collins's class? _____

7. Where do most of the averages fall? _____

8. What is the median (middle) average? _____

9. Compute the mean (average). _____

Total Problems:	Total Correct:	Score:

Name _____   Multiples and Factors

Study the box below. On the line provided, write the first 5 nonzero multiples of each number.

Rule:	Example:
The product of two whole numbers is a multiple of those numbers.	The first 5 nonzero multiples of 3 are: $3 \times 1 = \mathbf{3}$, $3 \times 2 = \mathbf{6}$, $3 \times 3 = \mathbf{9}$, $3 \times 4 = \mathbf{12}$, and $3 \times 5 = \mathbf{15}$.

1. 9 _9, 18, 27, 36, 45_
2. 6 _6, 12, 18, 24, 30_
3. 11 _11, 22, 33, 44, 55_
4. 25 _25, 50, 75, 100, 125_
5. 12 _12, 24, 36, 48, 60_
6. 21 _21, 42, 63, 84, 105_
7. 50 _50, 100, 150, 200, 250_
8. 100 _100, 200, 300, 400, 500_

Study the box below. List all of the factors of the given number.

Rule:	Example:
A factor is a number that is multiplied by another number to give a product.	$16 = 1 \times 16$, 2×8, 4×4 factors = **1, 2, 4, 8, 16**

9. 36 _1, 2, 3, 4, 6, 9, 12, 18, 36_
10. 75 _1, 3, 5, 15, 25, 75_
11. 63 _1, 3, 7, 9, 21, 63_
12. 49 _1, 7, 49_
13. 84 _1, 2, 4, 6, 14, 21, 42, 84_
14. 90 _1,2,3,5,6,9,10,15,18,30,45,90_
15. 42 _1, 2, 3, 6, 7, 14, 21, 42_
16. 56 _1, 2, 4, 7, 8, 14, 28, 56_

Total Problems: ___ Total Correct: ___ Score: ___   **9**

© Carson-Dellosa CD-2215

Name _____   Prime Factorization

Study the box below. In the space provided, make a factor tree to find the prime factorization of each number. Express the prime factorization using exponents.

Rule:	Example:
When a number is expressed as the product of all prime numbers, the expression is called **prime factorization**. A prime number has only two factors, 1 and the number itself. A **composite number** has more than two factors.	Factor tree: ... The prime factorization of 24 is **2 • 2 • 2 • 3**. Using exponents, it would be written $2^3 \cdot 3$.

1. 60 $2^2 \cdot 3 \cdot 5$ Factor trees may vary.
2. 81 3^4 Factor trees may vary.
3. 135 $3^3 \cdot 5$ Factor trees may vary.
4. 9 3^2
5. 39 $3 \cdot 13$
6. 150 $2 \cdot 3 \cdot 5^2$ Factor trees may vary.

10 Total Problems: ___ Total Correct: ___ Score: ___

© Carson-Dellosa CD-2215

Name _____   Greatest Common Factor

Study the box below. Find the greatest common factor (GCF) for each set of numbers. Write the answer in the space provided.

Rule:	Example:
List all of the factors of each number. Then, find the greatest factor common to both numbers. This will be the greatest common factor (GCF).	18, 24 18: 1, 2, 3, (6), 9, 18 24: 1, 2, 3, 4, (6), 8, 12, 24 GCF = 6

1. 56, 84 — 28
2. 8, 9 — 1
3. 14, 42 — 14
4. 48, 84 — 12
5. 78, 91 — 13
6. 40, 60 — 20
7. 18, 30, 42 — 6
8. 45, 60, 120 — 15
9. 15, 35, 70 — 5
10. $10ab, 25b^2$ — $5b$
11. $16x, 40x^2$ — $8x$
12. $9mn, 15m^2, 24mn^2$ — $3m$

Total Problems: ___ Total Correct: ___ Score: ___   **11**

© Carson-Dellosa CD-2215

Name _____   Least Common Multiple

Study the box below. Find the least common multiple (LCM) of each set of numbers. Write the answer in the space provided.

Rule:	Example:
List the multiples of each number. Stop when you have found the smallest multiple common of both numbers. This will be the least common multiple (LCM).	8, 12 8: 8, 16, (24) 12: 12, (24) LCM = 24

1. 10, 14 — 70
2. 24, 36 — 72
3. 18, 72 — 72
4. 2, 5, 8 — 40
5. 32, 64 — 64
6. 10, 25 — 50
7. 12, 16 — 48
8. 18, 32 — 288
9. 15, 24 — 120
10. 9, 12, 15 — 180
11. 7, 21, 84 — 84
12. 3, 5, 7 — 105
13. $10cd, 40d$ — $40cd$
14. $3y, 15y^2, 30$ — $30y^2$
15. $4x^2, 5x$ — $20x^2$

12 Total Problems: ___ Total Correct: ___ Score: ___

© Carson-Dellosa CD-2215

Worksheet 1 (page 13)

Name _____ Powers and Exponents

Study the box below. Follow the directions and write the answer in the space provided.

Rule:	Examples:	
An exponent tells the number of times a base is multiplied by itself. $9 \cdot 9 \cdot 9 \cdot 9 = 9^4$ → exponent → base	$4^3 = 4 \cdot 4 \cdot 4$	Expanded form
	$2 \cdot 4 \cdot 2 \cdot 4 = 2^2 \cdot 4^2$	Exponential form
	$5^2 = 25$	Simplified

Write each problem in expanded form.

1. 7^6
$7 \cdot 7 \cdot 7 \cdot 7 \cdot 7 \cdot 7$

3. x^3
$x \cdot x \cdot x$

5. $8^9 \cdot 9$
$8 \cdot 8 \cdot 8 \cdot 8 \cdot 8 \cdot 8 \cdot 8 \cdot 8 \cdot 8 \cdot 9$

2. 4^5
$4 \cdot 4 \cdot 4 \cdot 4 \cdot 4$

4. $a^2 \cdot b^2$
$a \cdot a \cdot b \cdot b$

6. $2^2 \cdot 3^5$
$2 \cdot 2 \cdot 3 \cdot 3 \cdot 3 \cdot 3 \cdot 3$

Write each problem in exponential form.

7. $5 \cdot 5$
5^2

10. $10 \cdot 9 \cdot 9 \cdot 10$
$10^2 \cdot 9^2$

13. $m \cdot n \cdot m \cdot m$
$m^3 \cdot n$

8. $11 \cdot 11 \cdot 11$
11^3

11. $2 \cdot 2 \cdot 4 \cdot 3 \cdot 3$
$2^2 \cdot 4 \cdot 3^2$

14. $x \cdot y \cdot x \cdot y$
$x^2 \cdot y^2$

9. $6 \cdot 6 \cdot 6$
6^3

12. $3 \cdot 2 \cdot 3$
$3^2 \cdot 2$

15. $a \cdot a \cdot a$
a^3

Simplify each problem.

16. 7^2
49

18. $2^5 \cdot 3^2 \cdot 4^3$
$18,432$

20. $12^2 + 9^2$
225

17. $4^4 + 3$
259

19. $8^2 \cdot 3^2$
576

21. $4^2 \cdot 6^3 \cdot 8^0$
$3,456$

© Carson-Dellosa CD-2215 | Total Problems: | Total Correct: | Score: | **13**

Worksheet 2 (page 14)

Name _____ Exponents

Study the box below. Simplify. Write the answers in exponent form in the space provided.

Rules:	Examples:
To multiply powers with like bases, add the exponents. Use the sum as the exponent with the base. To divide powers with like bases, subtract the exponents. Use the difference as the exponent with the base.	$4^4 \cdot 4^5 = 4^{4+5} = \mathbf{4^9}$ $\dfrac{3^6}{3^2} = 3^{6-2} = \mathbf{3^4}$

1. $2^3 \cdot 2^5$
2^8

7. $4^2 \cdot 4^2$
4^4

13. $x^3 \cdot x^6$
x^9

2. $5^8 \cdot 5^2$
5^{10}

8. $9^2 \cdot 9 \cdot 9^3$
9^6

14. $m \cdot m^3 \cdot m^4$
m^8

3. $8^3 \cdot 8^4$
8^7

9. $3 \cdot 3^4 \cdot 3^3$
3^8

15. $c^5 \cdot c^2$
c^7

4. $\dfrac{10^3}{10}$
10^2

10. $\dfrac{5^4}{5^4}$
5^0

16. $\dfrac{y^5}{y^4}$
y^1

5. $\dfrac{7^5}{7^4}$
7^1

11. $\dfrac{11^8}{11^5}$
11^3

17. $\dfrac{a^7}{a^4}$
a^3

6. $\dfrac{6^4}{6^2}$
6^2

12. $\dfrac{4^3}{4^2}$
4^1

18. $\dfrac{b^5}{b^4}$
b^1

14 | Total Problems: | Total Correct: | Score: | © Carson-Dellosa CD-2215

Worksheet 3 (page 15)

Name _____ Scientific Notation and Standard Form

Study the box below. Express each number in scientific notation. Write the answer in the space provided.

Rule:	Examples:
Scientific notation expresses numbers using powers of 10. Change the number (n) by moving the decimal point so that $1 \le n < 10$. Count the number of places the decimal point was moved. That number will become the power of 10 (positive if the decimal point moved to the left, negative if it moved to the right).	$301,000 = \mathbf{3.01 \times 10^5}$ $0.00532 = \mathbf{5.32 \times 10^{-3}}$

1. 0.000091
9.1×10^{-5}

4. 0.0000008
8.0×10^{-7}

7. 65,000
6.5×10^4

2. 2,700,000
2.7×10^6

5. 0.00083
8.3×10^{-4}

8. 402,000
4.02×10^5

3. 450,000,000
4.5×10^8

6. 72,000,000
7.2×10^7

9. 0.000000063
6.3×10^{-8}

Express each number in standard form.

Rule:	Examples:
Identify the power on the 10. For a positive power, move the decimal point that many places to the right. For a negative power, move the decimal point that many places to the left.	$9 \times 10^6 = \mathbf{9,000,000}$ $2.1 \times 10^{-6} = \mathbf{0.0000021}$

10. 7.15×10^4
$71,500$

13. 1.28×10
12.8

16. 4.3×10^7
$43,000,000$

11. 3.52×10^{-6}
0.00000352

14. 8.72×10^{-10}
0.000000000872

17. 6.4×10^{-5}
0.000064

12. 5×10^{-8}
0.00000005

15. 2.6×10^{-3}
0.0026

18. 4×10^{-7}
0.0000004

© Carson-Dellosa CD-2215 | Total Problems: | Total Correct: | Score: | **15**

Worksheet 4 (page 16)

Name _____ Squares and Square Roots

Study the box below. Find the square of each number. Write the answer in the space provided.

Rule:	Example:
To find the square of a number, multiply it by itself.	$8^2 = 8 \times 8 = \mathbf{64}$

1. 5^2 $\underline{25}$
4. 1^2 $\underline{1}$
7. 21^2 441
10. 18^2 324
13. 13^2 169

2. 7^2 $\underline{49}$
5. 3^2 $\underline{9}$
8. 6^2 36
11. 10^2 100
14. 20^2 400

3. 2^2 $\underline{4}$
6. 12^2 144
9. 15^2 225
12. 24^2 576
15. 16^2 256

Study the box below. Find each square root. Write the answer in the space provided.

Rule:	Example:
A radical sign, $\sqrt{}$, is the symbol used to indicate a nonnegative square root.	$\sqrt{16} = \mathbf{4}$ Since $4^2 = 16$, 4 is the square root of 16.

16. $\sqrt{81}$ 9
19. $\sqrt{169}$ 13
22. $\sqrt{324}$ 18
25. $\sqrt{361}$ 19
28. $\sqrt{289}$ 17

17. $\sqrt{36}$ 6
20. $\sqrt{1}$ 1
23. $\sqrt{225}$ 15
26. $\sqrt{625}$ 25
29. $\sqrt{0.16}$ 0.4

18. $\sqrt{9}$ 3
21. $\sqrt{196}$ 14
24. $\sqrt{100}$ 10
27. $\sqrt{256}$ 16
30. $\sqrt{0.04}$ 0.2

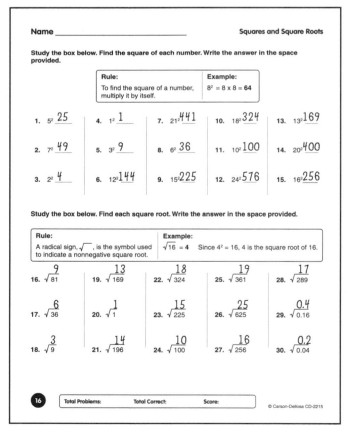

16 | Total Problems: | Total Correct: | Score: | © Carson-Dellosa CD-2215

Worksheet 17 — Order of Operations

Name _____ Order of Operations

Study the box below. Find the value of each expression. Write the answer on the line provided.

Rule:	Examples:	
Order of Operations: 1. Work inside all grouping symbols. 2. Compute all exponents. 3. Multiply and divide from left to right. 4. Add and subtract from left to right.	$24 - 2^2 \cdot 3$ $24 - 4 \cdot 3$ $24 - 12$ **12**	$2 \cdot (3 + 5) - 7$ $2 \cdot 8 - 7$ $16 - 7$ **9**

1. $12 \div 4 + 12 \div 3$
   7

2. $21 \div 3 + 4 \cdot 9$
   43

3. $27 \div 3^2 + 5$
   8

4. $6 \cdot 3 \div 2 - 1$
   8

5. $(9 + 6) \div 3$
   5

6. $9 + 6 \div 3$
   11

7. $76 - 7 \cdot 2^3$
   20

8. $(16 - 7) \cdot 2$
   18

9. $24 \div 4 - 3 \cdot 2$
   0

10. $(10 - 2)^2 \cdot 2$
    128

11. $10 - 2^2 \cdot 2$
    2

12. $2^2 \cdot 10 \div 5 + 3$
    11

13. $2[6(9 - 3)] - 20$
    52

14. $6[(9 + 5) - 2(3)]$
    48

15. $(8 - 5)^2 + 9 \div 3$
    12

16. $\dfrac{46 - 4}{7}$
    6

17. $\dfrac{16 + 8}{2^2}$
    6

18. $\dfrac{27 + 3}{3^2}$
    1

Total Problems: _____ Total Correct: _____ Score: _____ **17**

© Carson-Dellosa CD-2215

Worksheet 18 — Problem Solving

Name _____ Problem Solving

Solve each problem. Show your work and write the answer in the space provided.

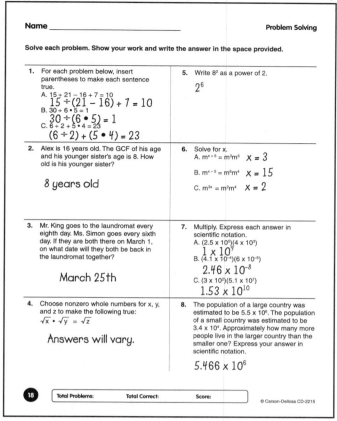

1. For each problem below, insert parentheses to make each sentence true.
   A. $15 \div 21 - 16 + 7 = 10$
   $15 \div (21 - 16) + 7 = 10$
   B. $30 \div 6 \cdot 5 = 1$
   $30 \div (6 \cdot 5) = 1$
   C. $6 \div 2 + 5 \cdot 4 = 23$
   $(6 \div 2) + (5 \cdot 4) = 23$

2. Alex is 16 years old. The GCF of his age and his younger sister's age is 8. How old is his younger sister?
   8 years old

3. Mr. King goes to the laundromat every eighth day. Ms. Simon goes every sixth day. If they are both there on March 1, on what date will they both be back in the laundromat together?
   March 25th

4. Choose nonzero whole numbers for x, y, and z to make the following true:
   $\sqrt{x} \cdot \sqrt{y} = \sqrt{z}$
   Answers will vary.

5. Write 8^2 as a power of 2.
   2^6

6. Solve for x.
   A. $m^{x+5} = m^3 m^5$ $x = 3$
   B. $m^{x-5} = m^6 m^4$ $x = 15$
   C. $m^{3x} = m^2 m^4$ $x = 2$

7. Multiply. Express each answer in scientific notation.
   A. $(2.5 \times 10^5)(4 \times 10^3)$
   1×10^9
   B. $(4.1 \times 10^{-4})(6 \times 10^{-5})$
   2.46×10^{-8}
   C. $(3 \times 10^2)(5.1 \times 10^7)$
   1.53×10^{10}

8. The population of a large country was estimated to be 5.5×10^6. The population of a small country was estimated to be 3.4×10^4. Approximately how many more people live in the larger country than the smaller one? Express your answer in scientific notation.
   5.466×10^6

18 Total Problems: _____ Total Correct: _____ Score: _____

© Carson-Dellosa CD-2215

Worksheet 19 — Integers and Absolute Value

Name _____ Integers and Absolute Value

Study the box below. Graph each set of numbers on a number line in the space provided.

Rule:	Example:
An **integer** is a whole number, a negative whole number, or 0.	Negative Integers Positive Integers $-3\ -2\ -1\ \ 0\ \ 1\ \ 2\ \ 3$

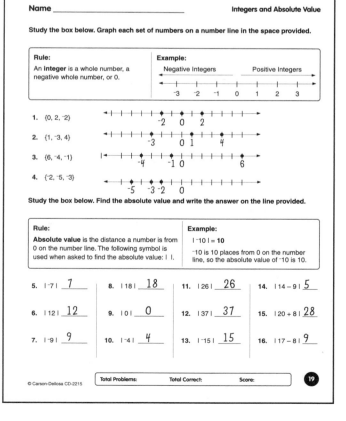

1. $\{0, 2, -2\}$
2. $\{1, -3, 4\}$
3. $\{6, -4, -1\}$
4. $\{-2, -5, -3\}$

Study the box below. Find the absolute value and write the answer on the line provided.

Rule:	Example:
Absolute value is the distance a number is from 0 on the number line. The following symbol is used when asked to find the absolute value: | |.	|−10| = **10** −10 is 10 places from 0 on the number line, so the absolute value of −10 is 10.

5. $|-7|$ **7**
6. $|12|$ **12**
7. $|-9|$ **9**
8. $|18|$ **18**
9. $|0|$ **0**
10. $|-4|$ **4**
11. $|26|$ **26**
12. $|37|$ **37**
13. $|-15|$ **15**
14. $|14 - 9|$ **5**
15. $|20 + 8|$ **28**
16. $|17 - 8|$ **9**

Total Problems: _____ Total Correct: _____ Score: _____ **19**

© Carson-Dellosa CD-2215

Worksheet 20 — Comparing and Ordering Integers

Name _____ Comparing and Ordering Integers

Study the box below. Compare using <, >, or =. Write the answer in the box provided.

Rule:	Example:
You can use a number line to compare integers. Values increase as you move to the right on the number line.	$2\ \boxed{>}\ -1$ 2 is farther to the right, so $2 > -1$. $-3\ -2\ -1\ \ 0\ \ 1\ \ 2\ \ 3$

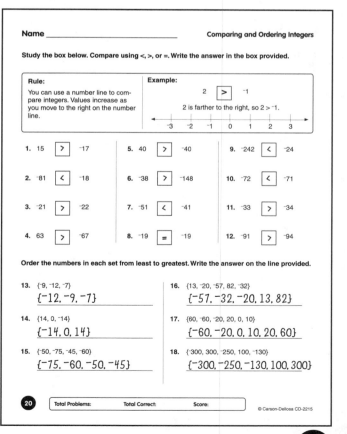

1. $15\ \boxed{>}\ -17$
2. $-81\ \boxed{<}\ -18$
3. $-21\ \boxed{>}\ -22$
4. $63\ \boxed{>}\ -67$
5. $40\ \boxed{>}\ -40$
6. $-38\ \boxed{>}\ -148$
7. $-51\ \boxed{<}\ -41$
8. $-19\ \boxed{=}\ -19$
9. $-242\ \boxed{<}\ -24$
10. $-72\ \boxed{<}\ -71$
11. $-33\ \boxed{>}\ -34$
12. $-91\ \boxed{>}\ -94$

Order the numbers in each set from least to greatest. Write the answer on the line provided.

13. $\{-9, -12, -7\}$
    $\{-12, -9, -7\}$

14. $\{14, 0, -14\}$
    $\{-14, 0, 14\}$

15. $\{-50, -75, -45, -60\}$
    $\{-75, -60, -50, -45\}$

16. $\{13, -20, -57, 82, -32\}$
    $\{-57, -32, -20, 13, 82\}$

17. $\{60, -60, -20, 20, 0, 10\}$
    $\{-60, -20, 0, 10, 20, 60\}$

18. $\{-300, 300, -250, 100, -130\}$
    $\{-300, -250, -130, 100, 300\}$

20 Total Problems: _____ Total Correct: _____ Score: _____

© Carson-Dellosa CD-2215

Name _____   Adding Integers

Study the box below. Find each sum. Write the answer in the space provided.

Rules:	Examples:	
The sum of two postive integers is positive.	19 + 5 = **24**	‾12 + 15
The sum of two negative integers is negative.	‾11 + ‾10 = **‾21**	I‾12 I = 12
When one integer is postive and one integer is negative, subtract the smaller absolute value from the larger absolute value. Give the result the sign of the integer with the greater absolute value.		I 15 I = 15
		15 – 12 = 3
		‾12 + 15 = **3**

1. 14 + (‾7)
   7

2. (‾20) + (‾5)
   ‾25

3. (‾18) + (‾4)
   ‾22

4. ‾9 + 25
   16

5. 15 + (‾31)
   ‾16

6. ‾20 + 7
   ‾13

7. ‾31 + (‾53)
   ‾84

8. 47 + 63
   110

9. 14 + (‾22) + 45
   37

10. ‾37 + (‾51) + 24
   ‾64

11. ‾27 + 41 + 16
   30

12. 71 + (‾71)
   0

13. 51 + (‾12 + ‾12)
   27

14. ‾25 + 5 + (‾10)
   ‾30

15. ‾14 + 14 + 63
   63

16. ‾17 + 16 + (‾15)
   ‾16

17. ‾27 + 31 + (‾19)
   ‾15

18. 41 + (‾41) + 41
   41

| Total Problems: | Total Correct: | Score: | **21** |

© Carson-Dellosa CD-2215

Name _____   Subtracting Integers

Study the box below. Subtract. Write the answer on the line provided.

Rule:	Examples:	
To subtract an integer, add its opposite.	‾15 – (‾9)	‾14 – 21
	‾15 + 9 = **‾6**	‾14 + ‾21 = **‾35**

1. ‾7 – 15   **‾22**
2. 14 – 20   **‾6**
3. ‾15 – 10   **‾25**
4. 18 – 21   **‾3**
5. 37 – (‾14)   **51**
6. 17 – 15   **2**
7. ‾11 – 6   **‾17**
8. 13 – 27   **‾14**

9. 40 – (‾14)   **54**
10. ‾35 – 35   **‾70**
11. ‾35 – (‾35)   **0**
12. 15 – (‾20)   **35**
13. 31 – (‾15)   **46**
14. 28 – (‾18)   **46**
15. ‾36 – 20   **‾56**
16. 33 – (‾16)   **49**

17. ‾57 – 27   **‾84**
18. ‾43 – 22   **‾65**
19. ‾17 – (‾30)   **13**
20. ‾73 – 63   **‾136**
21. 90 – (‾1)   **91**
22. ‾58 – 58   **‾116**
23. 61 – (‾61)   **122**
24. 46 – (‾56)   **102**

| **22** | Total Problems: | Total Correct: | Score: |

© Carson-Dellosa CD-2215

Name _____   Multiplying and Dividing Integers

Study the box below. Find each product or quotient. Write the answer on the line provided.

Rules:	Examples:		
The product or quotient of two integers with the same sign is positive.	‾5 • ‾8 = **40**	4 • ‾4 = **‾16**	(100 ÷ ‾5) • ‾2
The product or quotient of two integers with different signs is negative.	24 ÷ 6 = **4**	‾72 ÷ 8 = **‾9**	(‾20) • ‾2 = **40**

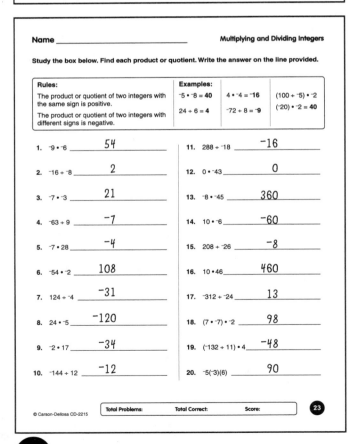

1. ‾9 • ‾6   **54**
2. ‾16 ÷ ‾8   **2**
3. ‾7 • ‾3   **21**
4. ‾63 ÷ 9   **‾7**
5. ‾7 • 28   **‾4**
6. ‾54 • ‾2   **108**
7. 124 ÷ ‾4   **‾31**
8. 24 • ‾5   **‾120**
9. ‾2 • 17   **‾34**
10. ‾144 ÷ 12   **‾12**

11. 288 ÷ ‾18   **‾16**
12. 0 • ‾43   **0**
13. ‾8 • ‾45   **360**
14. 10 • ‾6   **‾60**
15. 208 ÷ ‾26   **‾8**
16. 10 • 46   **460**
17. ‾312 ÷ ‾24   **13**
18. (7 • ‾7) • ‾2   **98**
19. (‾132 ÷ 11) • 4   **‾48**
20. ‾5(‾3)(6)   **90**

| Total Problems: | Total Correct: | Score: | **23** |

© Carson-Dellosa CD-2215

Name _____   Problem Solving with Integers

Solve each problem. Show your work and write the answer in the space provided.

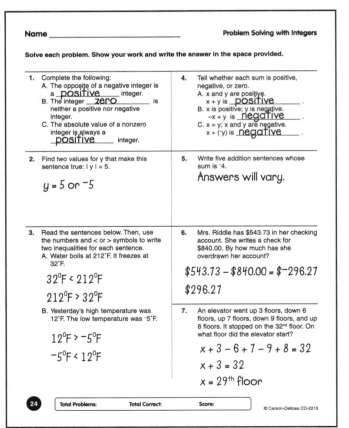

1. Complete the following:
   A. The opposite of a negative integer is a **positive** integer.
   B. The integer **zero** is neither a positive nor negative integer.
   C. The absolute value of a nonzero integer is always a **positive** integer.

2. Find two values for y that make this sentence true: I y I = 5.
   $y = 5$ or $‾5$

3. Read the sentences below. Then, use the numbers and < or > symbols to write two inequalities for each sentence.
   A. Water boils at 212˚F. It freezes at 32˚F.
   $32°F < 212°F$
   $212°F > 32°F$
   B. Yesterday's high temperature was 12˚F. The low temperature was ‾5˚F.
   $12°F > ‾5°F$
   $‾5°F < 12°F$

4. Tell whether each sum is positive, negative, or zero.
   A. x and y are positive.
   x + y is **positive**
   B. x is positive; y is negative.
   ‾x + y is **negative**
   C. x = y; x and y are negative.
   x + (‾y) is **negative**

5. Write five addition sentences whose sum is ‾4.
   Answers will vary.

6. Mrs. Riddle has $543.73 in her checking account. She writes a check for $840.00. By how much has she overdrawn her account?
   $543.73 – $840.00 = $‾296.27
   $296.27

7. An elevator went up 3 floors, down 6 floors, up 7 floors, down 9 floors, and up 8 floors. It stopped on the 32nd floor. On what floor did the elevator start?
   $x + 3 – 6 + 7 – 9 + 8 = 32$
   $x + 3 = 32$
   $x = 29th$ floor

| **24** | Total Problems: | Total Correct: | Score: |

© Carson-Dellosa CD-2215

Simplifying Fractions

Name _____

Study the box below. Reduce each fraction to lowest terms. Write the answer in the space provided.

Rule:	Example:
To reduce a fraction to lowest terms, divide the numerator and denominator by their greatest common factor (GCF).	$\frac{20 \div 5}{25 \div 5} = \frac{4}{5}$

1. $\frac{18}{36} = \frac{1}{2}$ (÷18)

2. $\frac{12}{20} = \frac{3}{5}$ (÷4)

3. $\frac{28}{48} = \frac{7}{12}$ (÷4)

4. $\frac{17}{51} = \frac{1}{3}$ (÷17)

5. $\frac{9}{24} = \frac{3}{8}$ (÷3)

6. $\frac{16}{64} = \frac{1}{4}$ (÷16)

7. $\frac{49}{140} = \frac{7}{20}$ (÷7)

8. $\frac{52}{56} = \frac{13}{14}$ (÷4)

9. $\frac{3}{30} = \frac{1}{10}$ (÷3)

10. $\frac{70}{105} = \frac{2}{3}$ (÷35)

11. $\frac{60}{125} = \frac{12}{25}$ (÷5)

12. $\frac{45}{72} = \frac{5}{8}$ (÷9)

13. $\frac{6}{15} = \frac{2}{5}$ (÷3)

14. $\frac{15}{80} = \frac{3}{16}$ (÷5)

15. $\frac{78}{112} = \frac{39}{56}$ (÷2)

16. $\frac{34}{60} = \frac{17}{30}$ (÷2)

17. $\frac{12}{90} = \frac{2}{15}$ (÷6)

18. $\frac{124}{172} = \frac{31}{43}$ (÷4)

19. $\frac{88}{121} = \frac{8}{11}$ (÷11)

20. $\frac{11}{99} = \frac{1}{9}$ (÷11)

21. $\frac{144}{216} = \frac{2}{3}$ (÷72)

22. $\frac{245}{428} = \frac{245}{428}$ (÷1)

23. $\frac{105}{133} = \frac{15}{19}$ (÷7)

24. $\frac{42}{91} = \frac{6}{13}$ (÷7)

© Carson-Dellosa CD-2215   Total Problems: ___   Total Correct: ___   Score: ___   **25**

Rounding and Estimating Fractions

Name _____

Study the examples below. Round each fraction to the nearest whole number or one-half. Write the answer in the space provided.

Examples:		
$1\frac{1}{8} = 1$	$2\frac{3}{5} = 2\frac{1}{2}$	$4\frac{12}{13} = 5$
The numerator is much smaller that the denominator, so round down to the nearest whole number.	The numerator is about half of the denominator, so round to the nearest one-half.	The numerator and denominator are close in value, so round up to the nearest whole number.

1. $3\frac{18}{36} = 3\frac{1}{2}$

2. $8\frac{1}{15} = 8$

3. $3\frac{3}{17} = 3$

4. $6\frac{4}{9} = 6\frac{1}{2}$

5. $3\frac{7}{8} = 4$

6. $4\frac{7}{18} = 4\frac{1}{2}$

7. $7\frac{1}{9} = 7$

8. $9\frac{9}{11} = 10$

Study the box below. Estimate each sum or difference. Write the answer in the space provided.

Rule:	Example:
To estimate a sum or difference, round each fraction to the nearest whole number or one-half. Then, add or subtract.	$3\frac{4}{7} + 5\frac{1}{11} =$ $3\frac{1}{2} + 5 = 8\frac{1}{2}$

9. $6\frac{1}{5} - 3\frac{6}{7} =$
   $6 - 4 = 2$

10. $5\frac{3}{4} + 7\frac{7}{8} =$
   $6 + 8 = 14$

11. $4\frac{3}{8} - \frac{1}{10} =$
   $4\frac{1}{2} - 0 = 4\frac{1}{2}$

12. $9\frac{1}{9} + 3\frac{3}{7} =$
   $9 + 3\frac{1}{2} = 12\frac{1}{2}$

13. $8\frac{1}{15} - 4\frac{2}{3} =$
   $8 - 5 = 3$

14. $6\frac{5}{8} - 4\frac{1}{12} =$
   $6\frac{1}{2} - 4 = 2\frac{1}{2}$

26   Total Problems: ___   Total Correct: ___   Score: ___   © Carson-Dellosa CD-2215

Adding and Subtracting Fractions

Name _____

Study the box below. Find each sum or difference and reduce to lowest terms. Write the answer in the space provided.

Rule:	Example:
1. Change any mixed or whole number to an improper fraction. 2. Rewrite each fraction using the least common denominator (LCD). 3. Add or subtract. Reduce if necessary.	$-2\frac{1}{2} = \frac{-5}{2} = \frac{-25}{10}$ $+\ 3\frac{1}{5} = +\frac{16}{5} = +\frac{32}{10}$ $\frac{7}{10}$

1. $2\frac{1}{2}$ $-\ \frac{1}{3}$ = $2\frac{1}{6}$

2. $4\frac{3}{8}$ $-\ 2\frac{1}{4}$ = $2\frac{1}{8}$

3. $-5\frac{7}{8}$ $-\ 2\frac{5}{6}$ = $-8\frac{17}{24}$

4. $-1\frac{7}{8}$ $+\ \frac{7}{12}$ = $-1\frac{7}{24}$

5. $3\frac{5}{12}$ $+\ 2\frac{1}{3}$ = $5\frac{3}{4}$

6. $4\frac{3}{10}$ $-\ 3\frac{1}{2}$ = $\frac{4}{5}$

7. $\frac{9}{10}$ $+\ 2\frac{1}{3}$ = $3\frac{7}{30}$

8. $12\frac{1}{5}$ $-\ 11\frac{7}{8}$ = $\frac{13}{40}$

9. $3\frac{5}{8} - (-2\frac{3}{5}) = 6\frac{9}{40}$

10. $3\frac{7}{10} + (-3\frac{7}{10}) = 0$

11. $12\frac{5}{8} - (-3\frac{2}{5}) = 16\frac{1}{40}$

12. $2\frac{1}{2} + (-3\frac{2}{7}) = \frac{-11}{14}$

© Carson-Dellosa CD-2215   Total Problems: ___   Total Correct: ___   Score: ___   **27**

Multiplying Fractions

Name _____

Study the box below. Find each product and reduce to lowest terms. Write the answer in the space provided.

Rule:	Example:
1. Change each mixed number or whole number to an improper fraction. If a numerator or denominator share a common factor, "cancel" by dividing the numerator and denominator by that factor. 2. Multiply the numerators. 3. Multiply the denominators.	$4 \times 2\frac{1}{2} =$ $\frac{\overset{2}{\cancel{4}}}{1} \times \frac{5}{\underset{1}{\cancel{2}}} = \frac{10}{1} = 10$

1. $\frac{1}{7} \times \frac{1}{8} = \frac{1}{56}$

2. $4\frac{1}{2} \times 8 = 36$

3. $\frac{3}{4} \times \frac{8}{9} = \frac{2}{3}$

4. $5 \times \frac{1}{10} = \frac{1}{2}$

5. $7\frac{7}{8} \times \frac{5}{9} = 4\frac{3}{8}$

6. $1\frac{1}{9} \times \frac{27}{40} = \frac{3}{4}$

7. $3 \times 1\frac{2}{3} = 5$

8. $-5 \times 2\frac{3}{4} = -13\frac{3}{4}$

9. $4\frac{1}{2} \times (\frac{3}{4})^2 = 2\frac{17}{32}$

10. $2\frac{2}{3} \times 2\frac{1}{5} = 5\frac{13}{15}$

11. $-3 \times (\frac{2}{5})^2 = \frac{-12}{25}$

12. $-2\frac{5}{6} \times 4\frac{2}{3} = -13\frac{2}{9}$

13. $\frac{2}{3} \times \frac{3}{4} \times \frac{2}{5} = \frac{1}{5}$

14. $2\frac{1}{4} \times 4 \times \frac{1}{3} = 3$

15. $\frac{-5}{2} \times \frac{5}{3} \times \frac{3}{5} = -2\frac{1}{2}$

28   Total Problems: ___   Total Correct: ___   Score: ___   © Carson-Dellosa CD-2215

Worksheet 29 — Dividing Fractions

Name _____ **Dividing Fractions**

Study the box below. Find each quotient and reduce to lowest terms. Write the answer in the space provided.

Rule:	Example:
1. Write any mixed or whole numbers as improper fractions.	$-15 \div \frac{3}{5}$
2. Multiply by the multiplicative inverse (reciprocal).	$\frac{-15}{1} \div \frac{3}{5}$
	$\frac{-15}{1} \times \frac{5}{3} = \frac{-45}{3} = -15$

1. $\frac{3}{4} \div 9 = \frac{1}{12}$

2. $\frac{6}{7} \div \frac{3}{8} = 2\frac{2}{7}$

3. $\frac{5}{12} \div \frac{4}{15} = 1\frac{9}{16}$

4. $-7\frac{1}{3} \div 1\frac{2}{9} = -6$

5. $5 \div \frac{-1}{4} = -20$

6. $\frac{15}{8} \div -3 = \frac{-5}{8}$

7. $-5\frac{2}{7} \div \frac{3}{8} = -14\frac{2}{21}$

8. $-7\frac{3}{5} \div -1\frac{9}{10} = 4$

9. $5\frac{1}{3} \div -2\frac{2}{3} = -2$

10. $4 \div -6\frac{2}{3} = \frac{-3}{5}$

11. $\frac{14}{11} \div \frac{16}{22} = 1\frac{3}{4}$

12. $\frac{5}{7} \div 5\frac{1}{14} = \frac{10}{71}$

13. $-1\frac{1}{2} \div \frac{3}{20} = -10$

14. $-2 \div \frac{-1}{3} = 6$

15. $-3\frac{1}{4} \div 2\frac{1}{6} = -1\frac{1}{2}$

| Total Problems: | Total Correct: | Score: | 29 |

© Carson-Dellosa CD-2215

Worksheet 30 — Problem Solving with Fractions

Name _____ **Problem Solving with Fractions**

Solve each word problem. Show your work and write the answer in the space provided.

1. Diane needs to purchase $1\frac{1}{2}$ yards of fabric for a shirt she is sewing and $3\frac{1}{2}$ yards of fabric for a sports jacket she is sewing. How many yards does she need in all?

$1\frac{1}{2} + 3\frac{1}{2} = 5$ yards

2. At the track meet, Jeremy cleared 4 feet $4\frac{1}{4}$ inches. Ronnie jumped $1\frac{1}{2}$ inches higher. How high did Ronnie jump?

4 feet + ($4\frac{1}{4} + 1\frac{1}{2}$) inches = 4 feet $5\frac{3}{4}$ inches

3. A unit fraction is a fraction that has a numerator of 1. Express $\frac{1}{3}$ as the sum of three unit fractions.

$\frac{1}{9} + \frac{1}{9} + \frac{1}{9} = \frac{1}{3}$

4. Marcus is typing a paper for his English class. The top margin must be a $\frac{1}{2}$ inch and the bottom margin must be $\frac{3}{4}$ inch. If the paper is 11 inches long, what is the length of the page inside the margin?

$11 - \frac{1}{2} - \frac{3}{4} = 9\frac{3}{4}$ inches

5. Sherry's mother told her she needed to roast her turkey $\frac{1}{4}$ hour for each pound. If she purchased a $13\frac{1}{2}$-pound turkey, how long would she have to roast it?

$\frac{1}{4} \cdot 13\frac{1}{2} = 3\frac{3}{8}$ hours

6. A recipe for a dozen muffins calls for $2\frac{1}{2}$ cups of flour. How much flour is needed to make half a dozen muffins?

$2\frac{1}{2} \div \frac{1}{2} = 1\frac{1}{4}$ cups

7. Katrina purchased a wooden board that was 18 feet long. If she needs to cut it into pieces that are 2 feet 6 inches long, how many pieces can be cut from the board?

$18 \div 2\frac{1}{2} = 7\frac{1}{5}$ pieces

8. Ronald is putting up a fence in his backyard. Each section of the fence is $5\frac{1}{2}$ feet long. If he installs 6 sections, how much fence has been installed?

$6 \cdot 5\frac{1}{2} = 33$ feet

| 30 | Total Problems: | Total Correct: | Score: | © Carson-Dellosa CD-2215 |

Worksheet 31 — Ratios and Rates

Name _____ **Ratios and Rates**

Study the box below. Use cross products to determine whether each pair of ratios is equal. Write "yes" or "no" on the line provided.

Rule:	Example:
A ratio is a comparison of two numbers. Cross multiply. If the cross products are equal, then the ratios are equal.	$\frac{2}{3}, \frac{8}{12}$ $2 \times 12 = 24$ $\frac{2}{3} \diagdown \frac{8}{12}$ $8 \times 3 = 24$ $24 = 24$, so, **yes, the ratios are equal.**

1. $\frac{4}{16}, \frac{8}{20}$ no

2. $\frac{21}{28}, \frac{3}{4}$ yes

3. $\frac{21}{49}, \frac{6}{14}$ yes

4. $\frac{6}{15}, \frac{3}{7}$ no

5. $\frac{16}{17}, \frac{8}{9}$ no

6. $\frac{12}{15}, \frac{4}{5}$ yes

7. $\frac{3}{11}, \frac{9}{33}$ yes

8. $\frac{2}{5}, \frac{14}{25}$ no

9. $\frac{2.1}{7}, \frac{1.4}{3.8}$ no

Study the box below. Express each rate as a unit rate. Round answers to the nearest tenth. Write the answer on the line provided.

Rules:	Examples:
A **rate** is simply a ratio of two measurements with different units.	rate: **$63 / 7 hours**
A **unit rate** is a rate in which the denominator is 1.	unit rate: **$63 ÷ 7 = $9 / 1 hour**

10. 1,150 words / 5 minutes _____ 230 words/1 minute

11. 30 days / 5 weeks _____ 6 days/1 week

12. 550 miles / 9 hours _____ 61.1 miles/1 hour

13. $.60 / 4 apples _____ $0.2/1 apple

| Total Problems: | Total Correct: | Score: | 31 |

© Carson-Dellosa CD-2215

Worksheet 32 — Proportions

Name _____ **Proportions**

Study the box below. Solve each proportion. Write the answer in the space provided.

Rule:	Example:
A **proportion** is two equivalent ratios. Cross products can be used to solve proportions.	$\frac{x}{27} = \frac{8}{6}$ $6 \cdot x = 27 \cdot 8$ $6x = 216$ $x = 216 \div 6$ **x = 36**

1. $\frac{4}{12} = \frac{y}{9}$ $y = 3$

2. $\frac{7}{16} = \frac{x}{32}$ $x = 14$

3. $\frac{9}{27} = \frac{5}{b}$ $b = 15$

4. $\frac{6}{x} = \frac{18}{24}$ $x = 8$

5. $\frac{4}{7} = \frac{x}{21}$ $x = 12$

6. $\frac{n}{2} = \frac{6}{15}$ $n = 0.8$

7. $\frac{10}{n} = \frac{12}{30}$ $n = 25$

8. $\frac{14}{22} = \frac{7}{m}$ $m = 11$

9. $\frac{27}{a} = \frac{18}{8}$ $a = 12$

10. $\frac{90}{45} = \frac{100}{x}$ $x = 50$

11. $\frac{x}{105} = \frac{7}{15}$ $x = 49$

12. $\frac{4}{9} = \frac{7}{y}$ $y = 15.75$

13. $\frac{a+1}{12} = \frac{2}{3}$ $a = 7$

14. $\frac{2}{6} = \frac{n+1}{9}$ $n = 2$

15. $\frac{12}{9} = \frac{y-3}{6}$ $y = 11$

| 32 | Total Problems: | Total Correct: | Score: | © Carson-Dellosa CD-2215 |

© Carson-Dellosa CD-2215

Worksheet 33 — Percents and Fractions

Name _____   Percents and Fractions

Study the box below. Write each fraction as a percent. Round to the nearest hundredth. Write the answer in the space provided.

Rule:	Example:
To change a fraction to a percent:	$\frac{5}{8}$
1. Change the fraction to a decimal. Divide the numerator by the denominator.	$5 \div 8 = .625$
2. Change the decimal to a percent. Multiply by 100, which moves the decimal point 2 places to the right. Add a 0 if necessary, and do not forget the percent sign.	**62.5%**

1. $\frac{27}{100} = $ **27%**
2. $\frac{7}{8} = $ **87.5%**
3. $\frac{9}{10} = $ **90%**
4. $\frac{3}{2} = $ **150%**
5. $\frac{8}{16} = $ **50%**
6. $\frac{3}{4} = $ **75%**
7. $\frac{2}{3} = $ **66.67%**
8. $\frac{5}{3} = $ **166.67%**
9. $1\frac{5}{8} = $ **162.5%**
10. $\frac{26}{20} = $ **130%**
11. $\frac{1}{125} = $ **0.8%**
12. $2\frac{1}{2} = $ **250%**

Study the box below. Write each percent as a fraction or mixed number in lowest terms in the space provided.

Rule:	Example:
To change a percent to a fraction:	$70\% = \frac{70}{100} = \frac{7}{10}$
1. Drop the percent sign and place the number over 100.	
2. Reduce to lowest terms.	

13. $35\% = \frac{7}{20}$
14. $5\% = \frac{1}{20}$
15. $74\% = \frac{37}{50}$
16. $1\% = \frac{1}{100}$
17. $91\frac{3}{4}\% = \frac{367}{400}$
18. $12\frac{1}{2}\% = \frac{1}{8}$
19. $10\frac{1}{4}\% = \frac{41}{400}$
20. $3\frac{1}{3}\% = \frac{1}{30}$

© Carson-Dellosa CD-2215   Total Problems: ___ Total Correct: ___ Score: ___   **33**

Worksheet 34 — Percents and Decimals

Name _____   Percents and Decimals

Study the box below. In the space provided, write each decimal as a percent.

Examples:	
0.72	3.09
$0.72 \times 100 = $	$3.09 \times 100 = $
72%	**309%**

1. $0.45 = $ **45%**
2. $0.08 = $ **8%**
3. $0.85 = $ **85%**
4. $0.9 = $ **90%**
5. $2.25 = $ **225%**
6. $0.035 = $ **3.5%**
7. $0.576 = $ **57.6%**
8. $0.004 = $ **0.4%**
9. $0.608 = $ **60.8%**
10. $3.456 = $ **345.6%**
11. $5.38 = $ **538%**
12. $0.57 = $ **57%**

Study the box below. In the space provided, write each percent as a decimal.

Rule:	Examples:	
To change a percent to a decimal:	31%	4%
Divide by 100 (which moves the decimal point 2 places to the left).	$31 \div 100 = $	$4 \div 100 = $
	0.31	**0.04**

13. $72\% = $ **0.72**
14. $9\% = $ **0.09**
15. $17\% = $ **0.17**
16. $90\% = $ **0.90**
17. $12.1\% = $ **0.121**
18. $200\% = $ **2.00**
19. $25\% = $ **0.25**
20. $\frac{1}{4}\% = $ **0.0025**
21. $\frac{3}{4}\% = $ **0.0075**
22. $10\frac{1}{2}\% = $ **.105**
23. $450\% = $ **4.5**
24. $80\% = $ **0.80**

34   Total Problems: ___ Total Correct: ___ Score: ___   © Carson-Dellosa CD-2215

Worksheet 35 — Estimating Percents

Name _____   Estimating Percents

Study the box below. Estimate. Write the answer in the space provided.

Rule:	Examples:	
One way to estimate percents is to change the percent to a close fraction and round the number.	40% of 62	8% of 12
	$\frac{2}{5} \times 60 = 24$	10% of 12
		$\frac{1}{10} \times 12 = $ **1.2**

1. 51% of 228 = $\frac{1}{2} \times 228 = 114$
2. 73% of 200 = $\frac{3}{4} \times 200 = 150$
3. 89% of 300 = $90\% \times 300 = 270$
4. 1% of 198 = $1\% \times 200 = 2$
5. 24% of 21 = $\frac{1}{4} \times 20 = 5$
6. 37% of 99 = $40\% \times 100 = 40$
7. 33% of 20 = $\frac{1}{3} \times 21 = 7$

8. 66% of 240 = $\frac{2}{3} \times 240 = 160$
9. 26% of 64 = $\frac{1}{4} \times 64 = 16$
10. 74% of 40 = $\frac{3}{4} \times 40 = 30$
11. 29% of 61 = $\frac{1}{3} \times 60 = 20$
12. 47% of $25.95 = $\frac{1}{2} \times 26 = 13$
13. 9% of 310 = $\frac{1}{10} \times 310 = 31$
14. 290% of 500 = $300\% \times 500 = 1,500$

15. 0.9% of 350 = $1\% \times 350 = 3.5$
16. 150% of 52 = $150\% \times 50 = 75$
17. 19% of 50 = $\frac{2}{10} \times 50 = 10$
18. 193% of 700 = $200\% \times 700 = 1,400$
19. 1.2% of 200 = $1\% \times 200 = 2$
20. 98% of 250 = $100\% \times 250 = 250$
21. 34% of 90 = $\frac{1}{3} \times 90 = 30$

© Carson-Dellosa CD-2215   Total Problems: ___ Total Correct: ___ Score: ___   **35**

Worksheet 36 — Percent of a Number

Name _____   Percent of a Number

Study the box below. Solve and round to the nearest tenth. Write the answer in the space provided.

Rule:	Example:
Percent Proportion: $\frac{Part}{Whole} = \frac{\%}{100}$	27 is 60% of what number?
Identify the part, whole, and/or percent.	$\frac{27}{x} = \frac{60}{100}$
Then, plug the numbers into the proportion and solve for the piece that is missing (part, whole, or percent).	$60x = 2,700$ $x = 45$ **27 is 60% of 45.**

1. 45 is 50% of what number?   **90**
2. Find 4% of $2,060.   **$82.40**
3. 65 is what percent of 98?   **66.3%**
4. 88 is 160% of what number?   **55**
5. What number is 6% of $9.40?   **$0.56**
6. 25% of 450 is what number?   **112.5**

7. 60 is what percent of 150?   **40%**
8. What number is 35% of 40?   **14**
9. What percent of 24 is 8?   **33.3%**
10. Find 70% of 80.   **56**
11. What number is 30% of 412?   **123.6**
12. What percent of 70 is 42?   **60%**

36   Total Problems: ___ Total Correct: ___ Score: ___   © Carson-Dellosa CD-2215

Worksheet 37 — Simple Interest

Name _____   Simple Interest

Study the box below. Find the interest and the total amount. Round to the nearest cent. Write the answer in the space provided.

Rule:	Example:
Simple Interest Formula: $I = prt$ I = interest p = principal r = rate t = time (expressed in years)	principal: $600 rate: $6\frac{1}{2}\%$ time: 9 months $I = 600 \cdot 0.0625 \cdot 0.75 = \mathbf{\$28.13}$ Total = interest + principal Total = $28.13 + $600.00 = **$628.13**

1. principal: $95
   rate: 18%
   time: 2 years

   $I = \$34.20$; Total = $129.20

2. principal: $400
   rate: 1%
   time: 6 months

   $I = \$2.00$; Total = $402.00

3. principal: $2500
   rate: 12%
   time: 3 years

   $I = \$900.00$; Total = $3,400.00

4. principal: $70
   rate: 2%
   time: 3 months

   $I = \$0.35$; Total = $70.35

5. principal: $695
   rate: 5%
   time: 15 months

   $I = \$43.44$; Total = $738.44

6. principal: $425
   rate: 10%
   time: 4 years

   $I = \$170.00$; Total = $595.00

7. principal: $90
   rate: 8%
   time: 21 months

   $I = \$12.60$; Total = $102.60

8. principal: $10,000
   rate: 12%
   time: 18 months

   $I = \$1,800.00$; Total = $11,800.00

Worksheet 38 — Problem Solving with Ratio and Percent

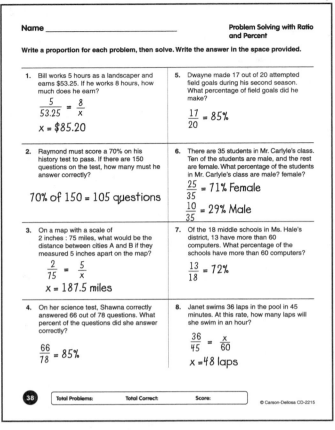

Name _____   Problem Solving with Ratio and Percent

Write a proportion for each problem, then solve. Write the answer in the space provided.

1. Bill works 5 hours as a landscaper and earns $53.25. If he works 8 hours, how much does he earn?

   $\frac{5}{53.25} = \frac{8}{x}$

   $x = \$85.20$

2. Raymond must score a 70% on his history test to pass. If there are 150 questions on the test, how many must he answer correctly?

   70% of 150 = 105 questions

3. On a map with a scale of 2 inches : 75 miles, what would be the distance between cities A and B if they measured 5 inches apart on the map?

   $\frac{2}{75} = \frac{5}{x}$

   $x = 187.5$ miles

4. On her science test, Shawna correctly answered 66 out of 78 questions. What percent of the questions did she answer correctly?

   $\frac{66}{78} = 85\%$

5. Dwayne made 17 out of 20 attempted field goals during his second season. What percentage of field goals did he make?

   $\frac{17}{20} = 85\%$

6. There are 35 students in Mr. Carlyle's class. Ten of the students are male, and the rest are female. What percentage of the students in Mr. Carlyle's class are male? female?

   $\frac{25}{35} = 71\%$ Female

   $\frac{10}{35} = 29\%$ Male

7. Of the 18 middle schools in Ms. Hale's district, 13 have more than 60 computers. What percentage of the schools have more than 60 computers?

   $\frac{13}{18} = 72\%$

8. Janet swims 36 laps in the pool in 45 minutes. At this rate, how many laps will she swim in an hour?

   $\frac{36}{45} = \frac{x}{60}$

   $x = 48$ laps

Worksheet 39 — Writing Algebraic Expressions

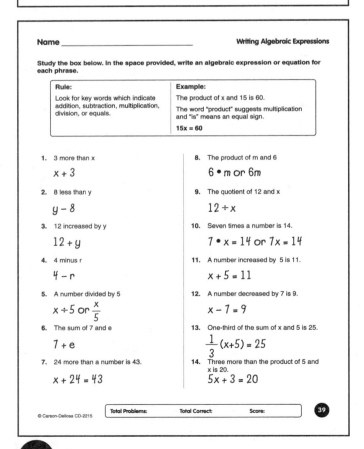

Name _____   Writing Algebraic Expressions

Study the box below. In the space provided, write an algebraic expression or equation for each phrase.

Rule:	Example:
Look for key words which indicate addition, subtraction, multiplication, division, or equals.	The product of x and 15 is 60. The word "product" suggests multiplication and "is" means an equal sign. **15x = 60**

1. 3 more than x

   $x + 3$

2. 8 less than y

   $y - 8$

3. 12 increased by y

   $12 + y$

4. 4 minus r

   $4 - r$

5. A number divided by 5

   $x \div 5$ or $\frac{x}{5}$

6. The sum of 7 and e

   $7 + e$

7. 24 more than a number is 43.

   $x + 24 = 43$

8. The product of m and 6

   $6 \cdot m$ or $6m$

9. The quotient of 12 and x

   $12 \div x$

10. Seven times a number is 14.

    $7 \cdot x = 14$ or $7x = 14$

11. A number increased by 5 is 11.

    $x + 5 = 11$

12. A number decreased by 7 is 9.

    $x - 7 = 9$

13. One-third of the sum of x and 5 is 25.

    $\frac{1}{3}(x+5) = 25$

14. Three more than the product of 5 and x is 20.

    $5x + 3 = 20$

Worksheet 40 — Evaluating Algebraic Expressions

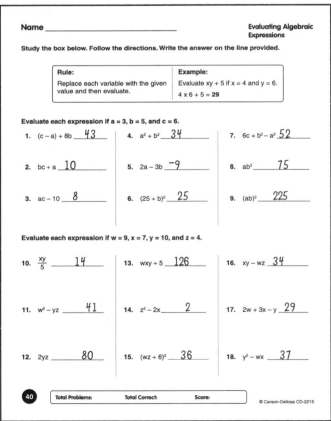

Name _____   Evaluating Algebraic Expressions

Study the box below. Follow the directions. Write the answer on the line provided.

Rule:	Example:
Replace each variable with the given value and then evaluate.	Evaluate xy + 5 if x = 4 and y = 6. 4 × 6 + 5 = **29**

Evaluate each expression if a = 3, b = 5, and c = 6.

1. $(c - a) + 8b$ __43__

2. $bc + a$ __10__

3. $ac - 10$ __8__

4. $a^2 + b^2$ __34__

5. $2a - 3b$ __−9__

6. $(25 + b)^2$ __25__

7. $6c + b^2 - a^2$ __52__

8. ab^2 __75__

9. $(ab)^2$ __225__

Evaluate each expression if w = 9, x = 7, y = 10, and z = 4.

10. $\frac{xy}{5}$ __14__

11. $w^2 - yz$ __41__

12. $2yz$ __80__

13. $wxy + 5$ __126__

14. $z^2 - 2x$ __2__

15. $(wz \div 6)^2$ __36__

16. $xy - wz$ __34__

17. $2w + 3x - y$ __29__

18. $y^2 - wx$ __37__

Addition and Subtraction Equations

Name _____

Study the box below. Solve and check each equation in the space provided.

Rules:
Solve each equation by using the inverse operation.

To check the equation, replace the variable with the solution.

Example:
$m - 2.4 = {}^-3.2$
$m - 2.4 + 2.4 = {}^-3.2 + 2.4$
$m = {}^-0.8$
Check: ${}^-0.8 - 2.4 = {}^-3.2$
$\phantom{Check: {}^-0.8 - 2.4 } {}^-3.2 = {}^-3.2$

1. $x + 76 = 89$
   $x = 13$

2. $m - 27 = 51$
   $m = 78$

3. $a + 12.4 = 9.2$
   $a = {}^-3.2$

4. $r - 41 = 27$
   $r = 68$

5. $b + 73 = 209$
   $b = 136$

6. $49 = y - 65$
   $y = 114$

7. $c + 6.2 = 8.5$
   $c = 2.3$

8. $p + 435 = 924$
   $p = 489$

9. $r - 64 = 157$
   $r = 221$

10. $x + 152 = 28$
    $x = {}^-124$

11. ${}^-120 = x + 59$
    $x = {}^-179$

12. $m - 4.6 = 7.7$
    $m = 12.3$

13. $b - 37 = {}^-61$
    $b = {}^-24$

14. $k + 18.3 = 29.1$
    $k = 10.8$

15. $306 = m + 198$
    $m = 108$

16. $74 = x + 137$
    $x = {}^-63$

17. $r + 30 = {}^-214$
    $r = {}^-244$

18. $142 = x - 38$
    $x = 180$

© Carson-Dellosa CD-2215 | Total Problems: | Total Correct: | Score: | **41**

Multiplication and Division Equations

Name _____

Study the box below. Solve and check each equation in the space provided.

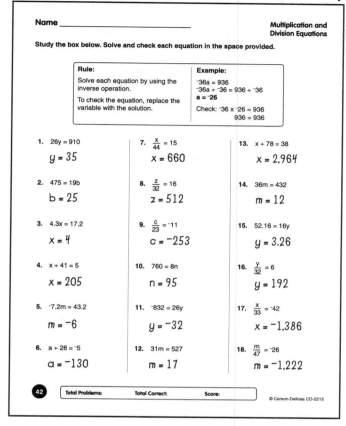

Rule:
Solve each equation by using the inverse operation.

To check the equation, replace the variable with the solution.

Example:
${}^-36a = 936$
${}^-36a \div {}^-36 = 936 \div {}^-36$
$a = {}^-26$
Check: ${}^-36 \times {}^-26 = 936$
$ 936 = 936$

1. $26y = 910$
   $y = 35$

2. $475 = 19b$
   $b = 25$

3. $4.3x = 17.2$
   $x = 4$

4. $\frac{x}{41} = 5$
   $x = 205$

5. ${}^-7.2m = 43.2$
   $m = {}^-6$

6. $\frac{a}{26} = {}^-5$
   $a = {}^-130$

7. $\frac{x}{44} = 15$
   $x = 660$

8. $\frac{z}{32} = 16$
   $z = 512$

9. $\frac{c}{23} = {}^-11$
   $c = {}^-253$

10. $760 = 8n$
    $n = 95$

11. ${}^-832 = 26y$
    $y = {}^-32$

12. $31m = 527$
    $m = 17$

13. $\frac{x}{78} = 38$
    $x = 2{,}964$

14. $36m = 432$
    $m = 12$

15. $52.16 = 16y$
    $y = 3.26$

16. $\frac{y}{32} = 6$
    $y = 192$

17. $\frac{x}{33} = {}^-42$
    $x = {}^-1{,}386$

18. $\frac{m}{47} = {}^-26$
    $m = {}^-1{,}222$

42 | Total Problems: | Total Correct: | Score: | © Carson-Dellosa CD-2215

Two-Step Equations

Name _____

Study the box below. Solve and check each equation in the space provided.

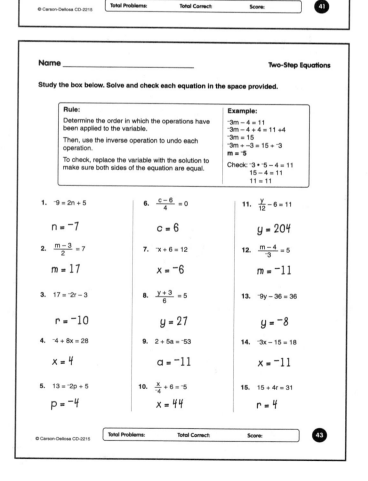

Rule:
Determine the order in which the operations have been applied to the variable.

Then, use the inverse operation to undo each operation.

To check, replace the variable with the solution to make sure both sides of the equation are equal.

Example:
${}^-3m - 4 = 11$
${}^-3m - 4 + 4 = 11 + 4$
${}^-3m = 15$
${}^-3m \div {}^-3 = 15 \div {}^-3$
$m = {}^-5$
Check: ${}^-3 \cdot {}^-5 - 4 = 11$
$ 15 - 4 = 11$
$ 11 = 11$

1. ${}^-9 = 2n + 5$
   $n = {}^-7$

2. $\frac{m-3}{2} = 7$
   $m = 17$

3. $17 = {}^-2r - 3$
   $r = {}^-10$

4. ${}^-4 + 8x = 28$
   $x = 4$

5. $13 = {}^-2p + 5$
   $p = {}^-4$

6. $\frac{c-6}{4} = 0$
   $c = 6$

7. ${}^-x + 6 = 12$
   $x = {}^-6$

8. $\frac{y+3}{6} = 5$
   $y = 27$

9. $2 + 5a = {}^-53$
   $a = {}^-11$

10. $\frac{x}{{}^-4} + 6 = {}^-5$
    $x = 44$

11. $\frac{y}{12} - 6 = 11$
    $y = 204$

12. $\frac{m-4}{{}^-3} = 5$
    $m = {}^-11$

13. ${}^-9y - 36 = 36$
    $y = {}^-8$

14. ${}^-3x - 15 = 18$
    $x = {}^-11$

15. $15 + 4r = 31$
    $r = 4$

© Carson-Dellosa CD-2215 | Total Problems: | Total Correct: | Score: | **43**

Solving Equations

Name _____

Study the box below. Solve and check each equation in the space provded.

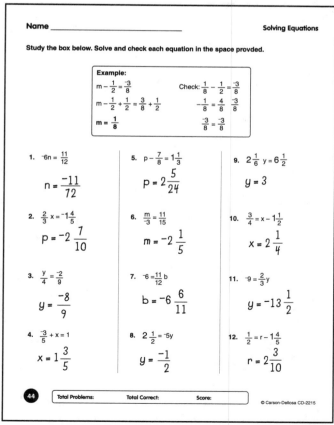

Example:
$m - \frac{1}{2} = \frac{{}^-3}{8}$
$m - \frac{1}{2} + \frac{1}{2} = \frac{3}{8} + \frac{1}{2}$
$m = \frac{1}{8}$

Check: $\frac{1}{8} - \frac{1}{2} = \frac{{}^-3}{8}$
$\frac{1}{8} - \frac{4}{8} = \frac{{}^-3}{8}$
$\frac{{}^-3}{8} = \frac{{}^-3}{8}$

1. ${}^-6n = \frac{11}{12}$
   $n = \frac{{}^-11}{72}$

2. $\frac{2}{3}x = {}^-1\frac{4}{5}$
   $p = {}^-2\frac{7}{10}$

3. $\frac{y}{4} = \frac{{}^-2}{9}$
   $y = \frac{{}^-8}{9}$

4. $\frac{{}^-3}{5} + x = 1$
   $x = 1\frac{3}{5}$

5. $p - \frac{7}{8} = 1\frac{1}{3}$
   $p = 2\frac{5}{24}$

6. $\frac{m}{3} = \frac{11}{15}$
   $m = {}^-2\frac{1}{5}$

7. ${}^-6 = \frac{11}{12}b$
   $b = {}^-6\frac{6}{11}$

8. $2\frac{1}{2} = {}^-5y$
   $y = \frac{{}^-1}{2}$

9. $2\frac{1}{6}y = 6\frac{1}{2}$
   $y = 3$

10. $\frac{3}{4} = x - 1\frac{1}{2}$
    $x = 2\frac{1}{4}$

11. ${}^-9 = \frac{2}{3}y$
    $y = {}^-13\frac{1}{2}$

12. $\frac{1}{2} = r - 1\frac{4}{5}$
    $r = 2\frac{3}{10}$

44 | Total Problems: | Total Correct: | Score: | © Carson-Dellosa CD-2215

Worksheet 45 — Combining Like Terms

Name _____ Combining Like Terms

Study the box below. Solve and check each equation in the space provided.

Rule:	Example:
1. Combine all like terms that have the same variable by adding or subtracting.	$54 = 3y + 6y$
	$54 = 9y$
2. Solve the equation for the variable.	$y = 6$
3. Check the equation by replacing each variable with the solution.	Check: $54 = 3 \cdot 6 + 6 \cdot 6$
	$54 = 18 + 36$
	$54 = 54$

1. $-121 = 3x + 8x$
   $x = -11$

2. $19v - 7v = -108$
   $v = -9$

3. $4b + 5b = 81$
   $b = 9$

4. $7x + x = 32$
   $x = 4$

5. $24x - 18x = 36$
   $x = 6$

6. $-65 = 13a - 8a$
   $a = -13$

7. $12m - 2m = 90$
   $m = 9$

8. $60 = 16y - y$
   $x = 4$

9. $7x - 4x = -45$
   $x = -15$

10. $6a + 12a = 108$
    $a = 6$

11. $-35 = -8x + 9x$
    $x = -35$

12. $9y - 2y = -63$
    $y = -9$

13. $28y - 14y = -42$
    $y = -3$

14. $8c + 9c = 51$
    $c = 3$

15. $-3a + 10a = 49$
    $a = 7$

16. $3.4m + 4.6m = 72$
    $m = 9$

17. $348 = 47h - 18h$
    $h = 12$

18. $43 = 6.2x + 2.4x$
    $x = 5$

© Carson-Dellosa CD-2215   Total Problems: ___ Total Correct: ___ Score: ___   **45**

Worksheet 46 — Simplifying to Solve Equations

Name _____ Simplifying to Solve Equations

Study the box below. Solve and check each equation in the space provided.

Rule:	Example:
Simplify all expressions in the equation by using the following properties:	$2(6n) + 12 + 4n = 60$
Commutative: the order of elements produces no change in the result.	$12n + 12 + 4n = 60$
	$16n + 12 = 60$
Associative: grouping two elements differently produces no change in the result.	$16n = 48$
	$n = 3$
Distributive: when a number is multiplied by a group of numbers, that number can be distributed to each number in the group.	Check: $2 (6 \cdot 3) + 12 + 4 \cdot 3 = 60$
	$36 + 12 + 12 = 60$
Then, solve the equation and check the solution.	$60 = 60$

1. $62 = 9y + 5(y+4)$
   $62 = 9y + 5y + 20$
   $y = 3$

2. $3(m - 1) + 4m = -73$
   $3m - 3 + 4m = -73$
   $m = -10$

3. $2(x + 9) + 3 = 45$
   $2x + 18 + 3 = 45$
   $x = 12$

4. $8c + 5(c - 6) = 9$
   $8c + 5c - 30 = 9$
   $c = 3$

5. $-b + 5 + 11b = -55$
   $10b + 5 = -55$
   $b = -6$

6. $4(m + 3) - 7m = 54$
   $4m + 12 - 7m = 54$
   $m = -14$

7. $20 = 14n - 9 + 3(5n)$
   $20 = 14n - 9 + 15n$
   $n = 1$

8. $-3(6x) - 8 + 4x = 76$
   $-18x - 8 + 4x = 76$
   $x = -6$

9. $4(c + 5) + 11c = 110$
   $4c + 20 + 11c = 110$
   $c = 6$

10. $8y + 9(y + 6) = 105$
    $8y + 9y + 54 = 105$
    $y = 3$

11. $-2(x + 3) + 6(-x) = 34$
    $-2x - 6 - 6x = 34$
    $x = -5$

12. $6(y - 4) + 2y + 8y = 72$
    $6y - 24 + 2y + 8y = 72$
    $y = 6$

46   Total Problems: ___ Total Correct: ___ Score: ___   © Carson-Dellosa CD-2215

Worksheet 47 — Variables on Both Sides

Name _____ Variables on Both Sides

Study the box below. Solve and check each equation in the space provided.

Rule:	Example:
When there are variables on both sides of the equation, move all of the variables to one side of equation and the numbers to the other side.	$6x = 24 + 2x$
	$6x - 2x = 24 + 2x - 2x$
	$4x = 24$
Then, solve the equation for the variable and check the solution.	$x = 6$
	Check: $6 \cdot 6 = 24 + 2 \cdot 6$
	$36 = 36$

1. $4y + 9 = 3y$
   $y = -9$

2. $8m = 5m + 18$
   $m = 6$

3. $16h = 72 + 7h$
   $h = 8$

4. $-4r + 15 = r$
   $r = 3$

5. $108 - 7x = -4x$
   $x = 36$

6. $63 + 9y = 16y$
   $y = 9$

7. $18b = 63 - 3b$
   $b = 3$

8. $3p + 9 = -15p$
   $p = \dfrac{-1}{2}$

9. $14f + 4 = 9f - 11$
   $f = -3$

10. $9m + 27 = 6m$
    $m = -9$

11. $4(x - 2) = 6x - 10$
    $x = 1$

12. $4(a + 2) = 2(a + 6)$
    $a = 2$

13. $\dfrac{1}{2}(x + 18) = 19$
    $a = 20$

14. $\dfrac{5}{6}y = \dfrac{1}{3}(y + 6)$
    $y = 4$

15. $\dfrac{5}{7}n + 12 = \dfrac{3}{7}n + 4$
    $n = -28$

© Carson-Dellosa CD-2215   Total Problems: ___ Total Correct: ___ Score: ___   **47**

Worksheet 48 — Inequalities

Name _____ Inequalities

Study the box below. Solve each inequality. Write the answer in the space provided.

Rule:	Examples:	
Solve an inequality the same way you would solve an equation. However, when multiplying or dividing by a negative number, reverse the sign of the inequality.	$y + 4 \geq -9$	$-2y < 10$
	$y + 4 - 4 \geq -9 - 4$	$-2y \div -2 < 10 \div -2$
	$y \geq -13$	$y > -5$
	Any number greater than or equal to -13 is a solution.	Any number greater than -5 is a solution.

1. $108 \geq -9b$
   $b \geq -12$

2. $-8 + a > 10$
   $a > 18$

3. $-30 \leq x + (-5)$
   $x \geq -25$

4. $\dfrac{x}{3} > -15$
   $x > -45$

5. $\dfrac{c}{7} < 12$
   $c < 84$

6. $12 > \dfrac{n}{5}$
   $n < 60$

7. $3y < -48$
   $y < -16$

8. $-27 < -3m$
   $m < 9$

9. $12 + x > -9$
   $x > -21$

10. $p + 13 > -13$
    $p > -26$

11. $-15 - y < 0$
    $y > -15$

12. $-6r \geq 72$
    $r \leq -12$

13. $7f + 3 > 52$
    $f > 7$

14. $4x - 7 \geq -35$
    $x \geq -7$

15. $2(x + 3) > 12$
    $x > 3$

16. $\dfrac{r}{2} - 5 > 27$
    $r < -64$

17. $\dfrac{m}{5} + 12 \geq 32$
    $m \geq 100$

18. $37 \leq \dfrac{a}{2} + 12$
    $a \geq 50$

48   Total Problems: ___ Total Correct: ___ Score: ___   © Carson-Dellosa CD-2215

Solving Inequalities

Name _____

Study the box below. Solve each inequality in the space provided.

Rule:	Example:
Solve inequalities with combined operations in the same way that you would solve an equation. Remember to reverse the sign of the inequality when multiplying or dividing by a negative number.	$-16 + 3a > -5a$ $-16 > -8a$ $2 < a$ $a > 2$ Any number greater than 2 is a solution.

1. $10 - 2y \leq -2$
$y \geq 6$

2. $-2 \geq -3x - 4$
$x \geq \dfrac{-2}{3}$

3. $2h + 1 < 13$
$h < 6$

4. $48 > -7m + 6$
$m > -6$

5. $4c - 7 > 21$
$c > 7$

6. $21 - 4x \leq 29$
$x \geq -2$

7. $\dfrac{a}{-20} > -3.7$
$a < 74$

8. $\dfrac{c}{5} + 26 \geq 51$
$c \geq 125$

9. $\dfrac{a}{-2} - 9 \leq 11$
$a \geq -40$

10. $-21 \geq 3 (b + 5)$
$b \leq -12$

11. $-2 (n - 4) \leq 10$
$n \geq -1$

12. $3 - 9x \leq 30$
$x \geq -3$

13. $13 \geq 3y - 5$
$y \leq 6$

14. $7 + 8y > 39$
$y > 4$

15. $4 \leq 2 (x - 6)$
$x \geq 8$

16. $10y - 5 > 4y - 3$
$y > \dfrac{1}{3}$

17. $-12m + 40 \leq 9m - 2$
$m \geq 2$

18. $5c - 21 < 11c + 9$
$c > -5$

| Total Problems: | Total Correct: | Score: | **49** |

© Carson-Dellosa CD-2215

Problem Solving with Algebra

Name _____

Solve each problem. Show your work and write the answers in the space provided.

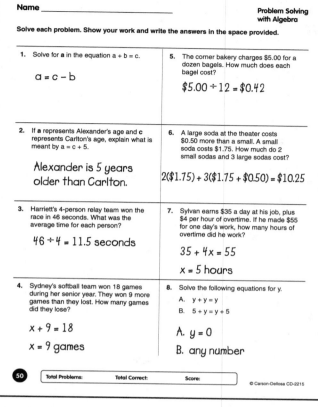

1. Solve for **a** in the equation $a + b = c$.
$a = c - b$

2. If **a** represents Alexander's age and **c** represents Carlton's age, explain what is meant by $a = c + 5$.
Alexander is 5 years older than Carlton.

3. Harriett's 4-person relay team won the race in 46 seconds. What was the average time for each person?
$46 \div 4 = 11.5$ seconds

4. Sydney's softball team won 18 games during her senior year. They won 9 more games than they lost. How many games did they lose?
$x + 9 = 18$
$x = 9$ games

5. The corner bakery charges $5.00 for a dozen bagels. How much does each bagel cost?
$\$5.00 \div 12 = \$0.42$

6. A large soda at the theater costs $0.50 more than a small. A small soda costs $1.75. How much do 2 small sodas and 3 large sodas cost?
$2(\$1.75) + 3(\$1.75 + \$0.50) = \$10.25$

7. Sylvan earns $35 a day at his job, plus $4 per hour of overtime. If he made $55 for one day's work, how many hours of overtime did he work?
$35 + 4x = 55$
$x = 5$ hours

8. Solve the following equations for y.
   A. $y + y = y$
   B. $5 + y = y + 5$
   A. $y = 0$
   B. any number

| **50** | Total Problems: | Total Correct: | Score: |

© Carson-Dellosa CD-2215

Introducing Polynomials

Name _____

Study the box below. Simplify. Write the answer in the space provided.

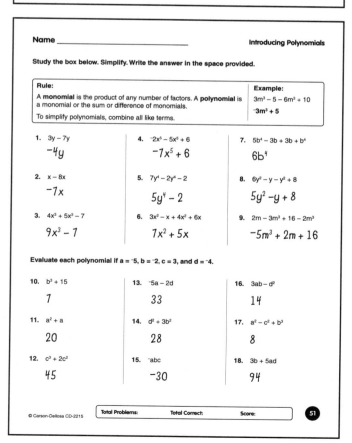

Rule:	Example:
A **monomial** is the product of any number of factors. A **polynomial** is a monomial or the sum or difference of monomials. To simplify polynomials, combine all like terms.	$3m^3 - 5 - 6m^3 + 10$ $-3m^3 + 5$

1. $3y - 7y$
$-4y$

2. $x - 8x$
$-7x$

3. $4x^3 + 5x^3 - 7$
$9x^3 - 7$

4. $-2x^5 - 5x^5 + 6$
$-7x^5 + 6$

5. $7y^4 - 2y^4 - 2$
$5y^4 - 2$

6. $3x^2 - x + 4x^2 + 6x$
$7x^2 + 5x$

7. $5b^4 - 3b + 3b + b^4$
$6b^4$

8. $6y^2 - y - y^2 + 8$
$5y^2 - y + 8$

9. $2m - 3m^3 + 16 - 2m^3$
$-5m^3 + 2m + 16$

Evaluate each polynomial if $a = -5$, $b = -2$, $c = 3$, and $d = -4$.

10. $b^3 + 15$
7

11. $a^2 + a$
20

12. $c^3 + 2c^2$
45

13. $-5a - 2d$
33

14. $d^2 + 3b^2$
28

15. $-abc$
-30

16. $3ab - d^2$
14

17. $a^2 - c^2 + b^3$
8

18. $3b + 5ad$
94

| Total Problems: | Total Correct: | Score: | **51** |

© Carson-Dellosa CD-2215

Adding Polynomials

Name _____

Study the box below. Add. Write the answer in the space provided.

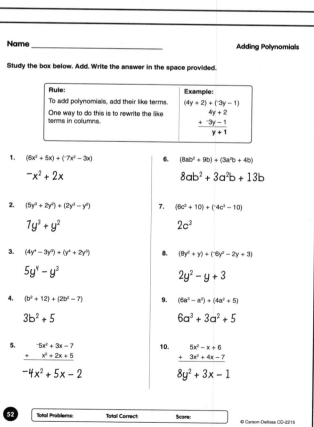

Rule:	Example:
To add polynomials, add their like terms. One way to do this is to rewrite the like terms in columns.	$(4y + 2) + (-3y - 1)$ $4y + 2$ $+ \ -3y - 1$ $y + 1$

1. $(6x^2 + 5x) + (-7x^2 - 3x)$
$-x^2 + 2x$

2. $(5y^3 + 2y^2) + (2y^3 - y^2)$
$7y^3 + y^2$

3. $(4y^4 - 3y^3) + (y^4 + 2y^3)$
$5y^4 - y^3$

4. $(b^2 + 12) + (2b^2 - 7)$
$3b^2 + 5$

5. $\begin{array}{r} -5x^2 + 3x - 7 \\ + \ x^2 + 2x + 5 \\ \hline \end{array}$
$-4x^2 + 5x - 2$

6. $(8ab^2 + 9b) + (3a^2b + 4b)$
$8ab^2 + 3a^2b + 13b$

7. $(6c^3 + 10) + (-4c^3 - 10)$
$2c^3$

8. $(8y^2 + y) + (-6y^2 - 2y + 3)$
$2y^2 - y + 3$

9. $(6a^3 - a^2) + (4a^2 + 5)$
$6a^3 + 3a^2 + 5$

10. $\begin{array}{r} 5x^2 - x + 6 \\ + \ 3x^2 + 4x - 7 \\ \hline \end{array}$
$8y^2 + 3x - 1$

| **52** | Total Problems: | Total Correct: | Score: |

© Carson-Dellosa CD-2215

© Carson-Dellosa CD-2215

Worksheet 53 — Subtracting Polynomials

Name _____   Subtracting Polynomials

Study the box below. Subtract. Write the answer in the space provided.

Rule:
To subtract polynomials, add their additive inverse.
It may be helpful to write the like terms in columns.

Example:
$(5x + 6) - (4x - 8)$
$5x + 6 + (^-4x + 8)$
$5x + 6$
$+ \ ^-4x + 8$
$x + 14$

1. $(6m + 5) - (m + 3)$

$5m + 2$

2. $(^-3a - 5) - (5a + 4)$

$^-8a - 9$

3. $(2x^2 + 2) - (3x^2 + 4)$

$^-x^2 - 2$

4. $(8b - 5) - (b + 9)$

$7b - 14$

5. $(4y^2 + 3y + 2) - (^-y^2 - 4y)$

$5y^2 + 7y + 2$

6. $(5 + 6y) - (3 - 2y)$

$8y + 2$

7. $(a^3 - 3a^2) - (4a^3 + 2a^2)$

$^-3a^3 - 5a^2$

8. $(3y^2 - 5y - 2) - (3y^2 + 6y - 8)$

$^-11y + 6$

9. $(5a + 6) - (^-6a + 8)$

$11a - 2$

10. $(3m^2 + 3m - 2) - (^-2m^2 + 2m - 5)$

$5m^2 + m + 3$

© Carson-Dellosa CD-2215   Total Problems: ___ Total Correct: ___ Score: ___   **53**

Worksheet 54 — Multiplying Polynomials

Name _____   Multiplying Polynomials

Study the box below. Find each product. Write the answer in the space provided.

Rule:
Use the distributive property to multiply a monomial by a polynomial.

Example:
$2y(3y + 4)$
$2y \cdot 3y + 2y \cdot 4$
$6y^2 + 8y$

1. $4x(2x + 5)$

$8x^2 + 20x$

2. $a(2a - 4)$

$2a^2 - 4a$

3. $2y(^-y + 4)$

$^-2y^2 + 8y$

4. $6b^2(^-3b + 2)$

$^-18b^3 + 12b^2$

5. $^-5x(^-3x^4 - 2x)$

$15x^5 + 10x^2$

6. $2y^3(y^3 + 4)$

$2y^6 + 8y^3$

7. $2x^2(3x^4 + 4x^3)$

$6x^6 + 8x^5$

8. $3a(^-3a^4b + a^2)$

$^-9a^5b + 3a^3$

9. $10y(^-y^4 - 2xy^2)$

$^-10y^5 - 20xy^3$

Study the box below. Find each product. Write the answer in the space provided.

Rule:
When multiplying two binomials, use the distributive property twice.

Example:
$(y + 2)(y^2 + 3)$
$y(y^2 + 3) + 2(y^2 + 3)$
$y^3 + 3y + 2y^2 + 6$
$y^3 + 2y^2 + 3y + 6$

10. $(a^2 - 4)(a - 5)$

$a^3 - 5a^2 - 4a + 20$

11. $(b^3 + 2)(b + 1)$

$b^4 + b^3 + 2b + 2$

12. $(c^4 - 2)(c + 4)$

$c^5 + 4c^4 - 2c - 8$

13. $(2x + 2)(2x + 3)$

$4x^2 + 10x + 6$

14. $(y - 6)(y + 6)$

$y^2 - 36$

15. $(xy + 3x^2)(xy - 3x^2)$

$x^2y^2 - 9x^4$

54   Total Problems: ___ Total Correct: ___ Score: ___   © Carson-Dellosa CD-2215

Worksheet 55 — Dividing Monomials and Polynomials

Name _____   Dividing Monomials and Polynomials

Study the box below. Find each quotient. Write the answer in the space provided.

Rule:
Divide by factoring the numerator and denominator, then cancel.

Example:
$\frac{6a^3}{3a} = \frac{2 \cdot \cancel{3} \cdot \cancel{a} \cdot a \cdot a}{\cancel{3} \cdot \cancel{a}}$
$2a^2$

1. $\frac{3b^2}{15b}$ \quad $\dfrac{b}{5}$

2. $\frac{16y^4}{4y^2}$ \quad $4y^2$

3. $\frac{35b^5}{5b^3}$ \quad $7b^2$

4. $\frac{9y^5}{9y^3}$ \quad y^2

5. $\frac{21a^4}{3a}$ \quad $7a^3$

6. $\frac{34x}{17}$ \quad $2x$

Study the box below. Find each quotient. Write the answer in the space provided.

Rule:
To divide a polynomial by a monomial, divide each term of the polynomial by the monomial, then simplify.

Example:
$(4b^2 - 8b + 12) \div 4$
$4b^2 \div 4 - 8b \div 4 + 12 \div 4$
$b^2 - 2b + 3$

7. $(24x^2 - 8x + 16) \div 8$

$3x^2 - x + 2$

8. $(12a^2 - 6a + 6) \div 6$

$2a^2 - a + 1$

9. $(5x^3 - 7x^2 + x) \div x$

$5x^2 - 7x + 1$

10. $(14c^3 - 21c^2 + 7c) \div 7c$

$2c^2 - 3c + 1$

11. $(18x^6 + 27x^4 + 9x^3) \div 9x^2$

$2x^2 + 3x + 1$

12. $(x^4 - 4x^3 + x^2) \div x^2$

$x^2 - 4x + 1$

© Carson-Dellosa CD-2215   Total Problems: ___ Total Correct: ___ Score: ___   **55**

Worksheet 56 — Coordinate System

Name _____   Coordinate System

To identify the coordinates of each point, use the coordinate system. Write in which of the quadrants each point lies.

1. A $(^-6, 6)$; II

2. B $(6, 4)$; I

3. C $(^-2, ^-4)$; III

4. D $(6, ^-6)$; IV

5. E $(^-6, 2)$; II

6. F $(^-8, ^-2)$; III

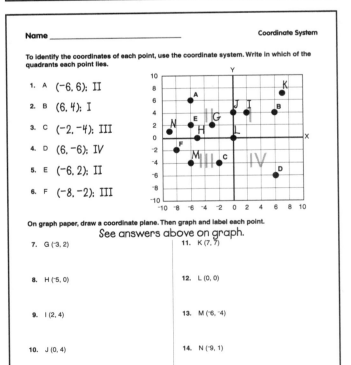

On graph paper, draw a coordinate plane. Then graph and label each point.

See answers above on graph.

7. G $(^-3, 2)$

8. H $(^-5, 0)$

9. I $(2, 4)$

10. J $(0, 4)$

11. K $(7, 7)$

12. L $(0, 0)$

13. M $(^-6, ^-4)$

14. N $(^-9, 1)$

56   Total Problems: ___ Total Correct: ___ Score: ___   © Carson-Dellosa CD-2215

Worksheet 57 — Graphing Inequalities on a Number Line

Name _____

Graphing Inequalities on a Number Line

Study the box below. Solve and graph the solutions on a number line in the space provided.

Rule:	Example:
Solve the inequality.	$3y - 4 < 2$
To graph the solution on a number line, shade the part of the number line indicated by the solution. A hollow circle indicates the solution is not included. A solid circle indicates the solution is included.	$3y - 4 + 4 < 2 + 4$ $3y < 6$ $3y + 3 < 6 + 3$ $y < 2$

This graph shows that $y < 2$.

1. $n - 1 > ^-6$ $n > ^-5$
2. $^-2h \le 6$ $h \ge ^-3$
3. $c + 8 \ge ^-2$ $c \ge ^-10$
4. $7m - 8 \le 20$ $m \le 4$
5. $3p - 9 > ^-24$ $p > ^-5$
6. $2r - 10 \ge 4$ $r \ge 7$
7. $5y - 3 \ge 12$ $y \ge 3$
8. $^-2d + 1 < 5$ $d > ^-2$
9. $^-3m + 6 \le ^-3$ $m \ge 3$
10. $^-2a + 4 \ge 6$ $a \le ^-1$

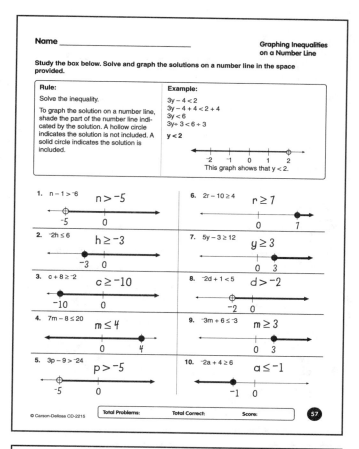

Total Problems: Total Correct: Score: **57**

© Carson-Dellosa CD-2215

Worksheet 58 — Equations and Ordered Pairs

Name _____

Equations and Ordered Pairs

Study the box below. In the space provided, make a table of solutions for each equation. Use values of $^-1$, 0, 1, and 3 for x. Write the solution as ordered pairs.

Rule:	Example:
The table should have 3 columns. Substitute each value of x for the expression in the middle of the table. Do the computation to find y.	$y = 2x + 1$

x	2x + 1	y
$^-1$	$2(^-1) + 1$	$^-1$
0	$2(0) + 1$	1
1	$2(1) + 1$	3
3	$2(3) + 1$	7

The ordered pairs are as follows:
$(^-1, ^-1); (0, 1); (1, 3); (3, 7)$

1. $y = x + 3$

$(^-1, 2)$
$(0, 3)$
$(1, 4)$
$(3, 6)$

x	x + 3	y
$^-1$	$^-1 + 3$	2
0	$0 + 3$	3
1	$1 + 3$	4
3	$3 + 3$	6

2. $y = 4x$

$(^-1, ^-4)$
$(0, 0)$
$(1, 4)$
$(3, 12)$

x	4x	y
$^-1$	$4(^-1)$	$^-4$
0	$4(0)$	0
1	$4(1)$	4
3	$4(3)$	12

3. $y = 2x - 3$

$(^-1, ^-5)$
$(0, ^-3)$
$(1, ^-1)$
$(3, 3)$

x	2x - 3	y
$^-1$	$2(^-1) - 3$	$^-5$
0	$2(0) - 3$	$^-3$
1	$2(1) - 3$	$^-1$
3	$2(3) - 3$	3

4. $y = ^-3x + 5$

$(^-1, 8)$
$(0, 5)$
$(1, 2)$
$(3, ^-4)$

x	$^-3x + 5$	y
$^-1$	$^-3(^-1) + 5$	8
0	$^-3(0) + 5$	5
1	$^-3(1) + 5$	2
3	$^-3(3) + 5$	$^-4$

5. $y = ^-3x - 1$

$(^-1, 2)$
$(0, ^-1)$
$(1, ^-4)$
$(3, ^-10)$

x	$^-3x - 1$	y
$^-1$	$^-3(^-1) - 1$	2
0	$^-3(0) - 1$	$^-1$
1	$^-3(1) - 1$	$^-4$
3	$^-3(3) - 1$	$^-10$

6. $y = 5x - 8$

$(^-1, ^-13)$
$(0, ^-8)$
$(1, ^-3)$
$(3, 7)$

x	5x - 8	y
$^-1$	$5(^-1) - 8$	$^-13$
0	$5(0) - 8$	$^-8$
1	$5(1) - 8$	$^-3$
3	$5(3) - 8$	7

58   Total Problems: Total Correct: Score:

© Carson-Dellosa CD-2215

Worksheet 59 — Graphing Linear Equations

Name _____

Graphing Linear Equations

Study the box below. Make a table of solutions and list the ordered pairs. Then, graph each equation.

Example:

$y = 2x + 2$

Table of Solutions

x	2x + 2	y
$^-1$	$2(^-1) + 2$	0
0	$2(0) + 2$	2
1	$2(1) + 2$	4
3	$2(3) + 2$	8

ordered pairs: $(^-1, 0); (0, 2); (1, 4); (3, 8)$

1. $y = x - 3$

$(^-1, 4)$
$(0, 3)$
$(1, ^-2)$
$(3, 0)$

x	x - 3	y
$^-1$	$^-1 - 3$	$^-4$
0	$0 - 3$	$^-3$
1	$1 - 3$	$^-2$
3	$3 - 3$	0

2. $y = ^-6x + 1$

$(^-1, 7)$
$(0, 1)$
$(1, ^-5)$
$(3, ^-17)$

x	$^-6x + 1$	y
$^-1$	$^-6(^-1) + 1$	7
0	$^-6(0) + 1$	1
1	$^-6(1) + 1$	$^-5$
3	$^-6(3) + 1$	$^-17$

3. $y = ^-2x + 2$

$(^-1, 4)$
$(0, 2)$
$(1, 0)$
$(3, ^-4)$

x	$^-2x + 2$	y
$^-1$	$^-2(^-1) + 2$	4
0	$^-2(0) + 2$	2
1	$^-2(1) + 2$	0
3	$^-2(3) + 2$	$^-4$

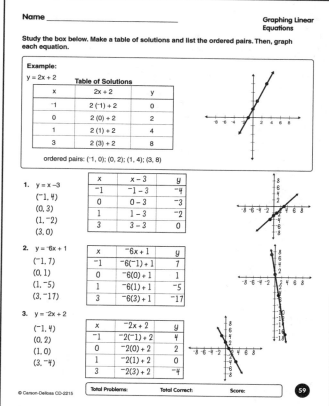

Total Problems: Total Correct: Score: **59**

© Carson-Dellosa CD-2215

Worksheet 60 — Slope

Name _____

Slope

Study the box below. Find the slope of each line given two points on the line.

Rule:	Example:
Slope is the steepness of a line. To find the slope, compute the change in y over the change in x.	$(^-4, ^-2); (5, 3)$ Change in y: $3 - (^-2) = 5$ Change in x: $5 - (^-4) = 9$ The slope is $\frac{5}{9}$.

1. $(^-4, ^-1); (^-2, 3)$
$$\frac{3 - (^-1)}{^-2 - (^-4)} = \frac{4}{2} = 2$$

2. $(^-2, 5); (1, 6)$
$$\frac{6 - 5}{1 - (^-2)} = \frac{1}{3}$$

3. $(5, 10); (^-2, ^-3)$
$$\frac{^-3 - 10}{^-2 - 5} = \frac{^-13}{^-7} = \frac{13}{7}$$

4. $(3, 2); (^-1, ^-4)$
$$\frac{^-4 - 2}{^-1 - 3} = \frac{^-6}{^-4} = \frac{3}{2}$$

5. $(6, 4); (^-2, 2)$
$$\frac{2 - 4}{^-2 - 6} = \frac{^-2}{^-8} = \frac{1}{4}$$

6. $(^-4, 3); (3, 4)$
$$\frac{4 - 3}{3 - (^-4)} = \frac{1}{7}$$

7. $(3, 4); (^-2, 3)$
$$\frac{3 - 4}{^-2 - 3} = \frac{^-1}{^-5} = \frac{1}{5}$$

8. $(^-2, 3); (1, ^-5)$
$$\frac{^-5 - (^-3)}{1 - (^-2)} = \frac{^-2}{3}$$

9. $(6, ^-3); (5, ^-3)$
$$\frac{^-3 - (^-3)}{5 - 6} = \frac{0}{^-1} = 0$$

10. $(2, 4); (5, 8)$
$$\frac{8 - 4}{5 - 2} = \frac{4}{3}$$

11. $(7, 3); (^-1, ^-3)$
$$\frac{^-3 - 3}{^-1 - 7} = \frac{^-6}{^-8} = \frac{3}{4}$$

12. $(^-3, 3); (3, ^-3)$
$$\frac{^-3 - 3}{3 - (^-3)} = \frac{^-6}{6} = ^-1$$

13. $(^-3, 7); (4, ^-6)$
$$\frac{^-6 - 7}{4 - (^-3)} = \frac{^-13}{7}$$

14. $(^-5, ^-7); (^-1, 3)$
$$\frac{3 - (^-7)}{^-1 - (^-5)} = \frac{10}{4} = \frac{5}{2}$$

15. $(^-3, ^-2); (3, 5)$
$$\frac{5 - (^-2)}{3 - (^-3)} = \frac{7}{6}$$

60   Total Problems: Total Correct: Score:

© Carson-Dellosa CD-2215

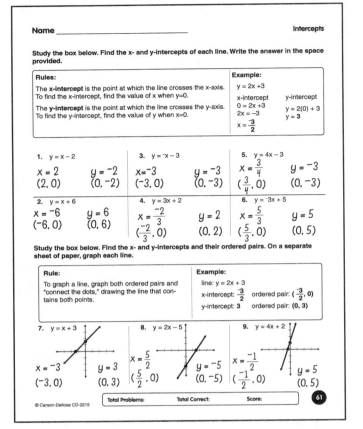

Intercepts (page 61)

Name _____ Intercepts

Study the box below. Find the x- and y-intercepts of each line. Write the answer in the space provided.

Rules:
The **x-intercept** is the point at which the line crosses the x-axis. To find the x-intercept, find the value of x when y=0.

The **y-intercept** is the point at which the line crosses the y-axis. To find the y-intercept, find the value of y when x=0.

Example:
$y = 2x + 3$

x-intercept	y-intercept
$0 = 2x + 3$	$y = 2(0) + 3$
$2x = -3$	$y = 3$
$x = \frac{-3}{2}$	

1. $y = x - 2$ $x = 2$ (2, 0) $y = -2$ (0, -2)
3. $y = -x - 3$ $x = -3$ (-3, 0) $y = -3$ (0, -3)
5. $y = 4x - 3$ $x = \frac{3}{4}$ $(\frac{3}{4}, 0)$ $y = -3$ (0, -3)

2. $y = x + 6$ $x = -6$ (-6, 0) $y = 6$ (0, 6)
4. $y = 3x + 2$ $x = \frac{-2}{3}$ $(\frac{-2}{3}, 0)$ $y = 2$ (0, 2)
6. $y = -3x + 5$ $x = \frac{5}{3}$ $(\frac{5}{3}, 0)$ $y = 5$ (0, 5)

Study the box below. Find the x- and y-intercepts and their ordered pairs. On a separate sheet of paper, graph each line.

Rule:
To graph a line, graph both ordered pairs and "connect the dots," drawing the line that contains both points.

Example:
line: $y = 2x + 3$
x-intercept: $\frac{-3}{2}$ ordered pair: $(\frac{-3}{2}, 0)$
y-intercept: 3 ordered pair: (0, 3)

7. $y = x + 3$ $x = -3$ (-3, 0) $y = 3$ (0, 3)
8. $y = 2x - 5$ $x = \frac{5}{2}$ $(\frac{5}{2}, 0)$ $y = -5$ (0, -5)
9. $y = 4x + 2$ $x = \frac{-1}{2}$ $(\frac{-1}{2}, 0)$ $y = 5$ (0, 5)

© Carson-Dellosa CD-2215 | Total Problems: | Total Correct: | Score: | **61**

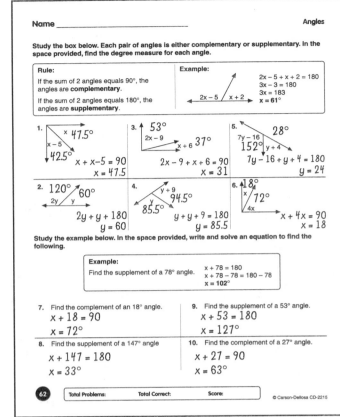

Angles (page 62)

Name _____ Angles

Study the box below. Each pair of angles is either complementary or supplementary. In the space provided, find the degree measure for each angle.

Rule:
If the sum of 2 angles equals 90°, the angles are **complementary**.

If the sum of 2 angles equals 180°, the angles are **supplementary**.

Example:
$2x - 5 + x + 2 = 180$
$3x - 3 = 180$
$3x = 183$
$x = 61°$

1. x 47.5° $x-5$ 42.5° $x + x - 5 = 90$ $x = 47.5$
3. 53° $2x-9$ $x+6$ 37° $2x - 9 + x + 6 = 90$ $x = 31$
5. $7y-16$ 28° 152° $y+4$ $7y - 16 + y + 4 = 180$ $y = 24$

2. 120° 60° $2y$ y $2y + y + 180$ $y = 60$
4. $y+9$ 94.5° 85.5° y $y + y + 9 = 180$ $y = 85.5$
6. 18° x 72° $4x$ $x + 4x = 90$ $x = 18$

Study the example below. In the space provided, write and solve an equation to find the following.

Example:
Find the supplement of a 78° angle.
$x + 78 = 180$
$x + 78 - 78 = 180 - 78$
$x = 102°$

7. Find the complement of an 18° angle.
$x + 18 = 90$
$x = 72°$

9. Find the supplement of a 53° angle.
$x + 53 = 180$
$x = 127°$

8. Find the supplement of a 147° angle
$x + 147 = 180$
$x = 33°$

10. Find the complement of a 27° angle.
$x + 27 = 90$
$x = 63°$

62 | Total Problems: | Total Correct: | Score: | © Carson-Dellosa CD-2215

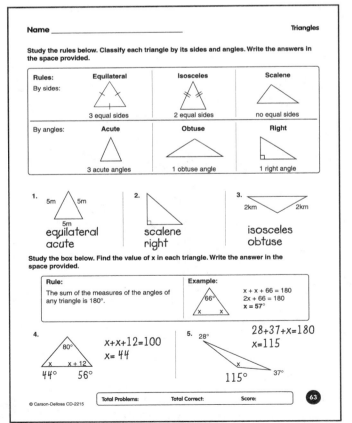

Triangles (page 63)

Name _____ Triangles

Study the rules below. Classify each triangle by its sides and angles. Write the answers in the space provided.

Rules:
By sides:
- Equilateral — 3 equal sides
- Isosceles — 2 equal sides
- Scalene — no equal sides

By angles:
- Acute — 3 acute angles
- Obtuse — 1 obtuse angle
- Right — 1 right angle

1. 5m 5m 5m — equilateral acute
2. scalene right
3. 2km 2km — isosceles obtuse

Study the box below. Find the value of x in each triangle. Write the answer in the space provided.

Rule:
The sum of the measures of the angles of any triangle is 180°.

Example:
$x + x + 66 = 180$
$2x + 66 = 180$
$x = 57°$

4. 80° x $x+12$ $x + x + 12 = 100$ $x = 44$ 44° 56°
5. 28° x 37° $28 + 37 + x = 180$ $x = 115$ 115°

© Carson-Dellosa CD-2215 | Total Problems: | Total Correct: | Score: | **63**

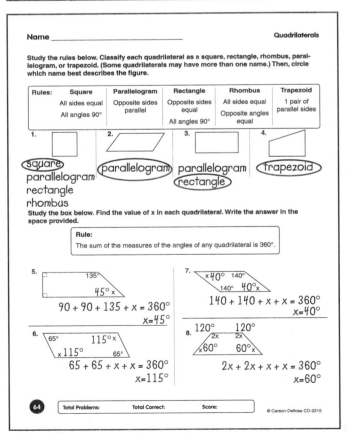

Quadrilaterals (page 64)

Name _____ Quadrilaterals

Study the rules below. Classify each quadrilateral as a square, rectangle, rhombus, parallelogram, or trapezoid. (Some quadrilaterals may have more than one name.) Then, circle which name best describes the figure.

Rules:

Square	Parallelogram	Rectangle	Rhombus	Trapezoid
All sides equal All angles 90°	Opposite sides parallel	Opposite sides equal All angles 90°	All sides equal Opposite angles equal	1 pair of parallel sides

1. (square) parallelogram rectangle rhombus
2. (parallelogram)
3. parallelogram (rectangle)
4. (trapezoid)

Study the box below. Find the value of x in each quadrilateral. Write the answer in the space provided.

Rule:
The sum of the measures of the angles of any quadrilateral is 360°.

5. 135° 45° x $90 + 90 + 135 + x = 360°$ $x = 45°$
7. x 40° 140° 140° 40° x $140 + 140 + x + x = 360°$ $x = 40°$

6. 65° 115° x 115° 65° $65 + 65 + x + x = 360°$ $x = 115°$
8. 120° 120° $2x$ $2x$ x 60° 60° x $2x + 2x + x + x = 360°$ $x = 60°$

64 | Total Problems: | Total Correct: | Score: | © Carson-Dellosa CD-2215

Pythagorean Theorem

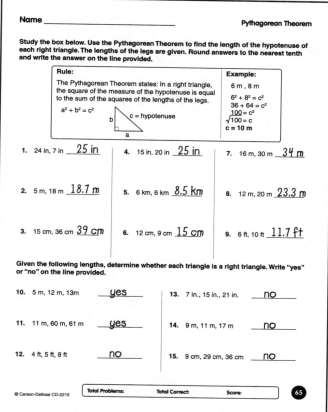

Name _____

Study the box below. Use the Pythagorean Theorem to find the length of the hypotenuse of each right triangle. The lengths of the legs are given. Round answers to the nearest tenth and write the answer on the line provided.

Rule:
The Pythagorean Theorem states: In a right triangle, the square of the measure of the hypotenuse is equal to the sum of the squares of the lengths of the legs.

$a^2 + b^2 = c^2$

c = hypotenuse

Example:
6 m , 8 m
$6^2 + 8^2 = c^2$
$36 + 64 = c^2$
$100 = c^2$
$\sqrt{100} = c$
c = 10 m

1. 24 in, 7 in __25 in__
2. 5 m, 18 m __18.7 m__
3. 15 cm, 36 cm __39 cm__

4. 15 in, 20 in __25 in__
5. 6 km, 6 km __8.5 km__
6. 12 cm, 9 cm __15 cm__

7. 16 m, 30 m __34 m__
8. 12 m, 20 m __23.3 m__
9. 6 ft, 10 ft __11.7 ft__

Given the following lengths, determine whether each triangle is a right triangle. Write "yes" or "no" on the line provided.

10. 5 m, 12 m, 13m __yes__
11. 11 m, 60 m, 61 m __yes__
12. 4 ft, 5 ft, 8 ft __no__

13. 7 in., 15 in., 21 in. __no__
14. 9 m, 11 m, 17 m __no__
15. 9 cm, 29 cm, 36 cm __no__

© Carson-Dellosa CD-2215 | Total Problems: | Total Correct: | Score: | **65**

Perimeter

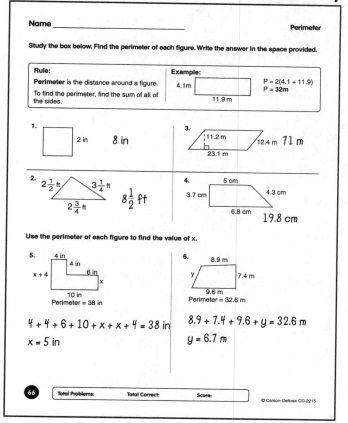

Name _____

Study the box below. Find the perimeter of each figure. Write the answer in the space provided.

Rule:
Perimeter is the distance around a figure. To find the perimeter, find the sum of all of the sides.

Example:
4.1m, 11.9 m
P = 2(4.1 + 11.9)
P = 32m

1. 2 in — **8 in**

2. $2\frac{1}{2}$ ft, $3\frac{1}{4}$ ft, $2\frac{3}{4}$ ft — $8\frac{1}{2}$ ft

3. 11.2 m, 23.1 m, 12.4 m — **71 m**

4. 5 cm, 3.7 cm, 4.3 cm, 6.8 cm — **19.8 cm**

Use the perimeter of each figure to find the value of x.

5. 4 in, 4 in, 6 in, x+4, x, 10 in
Perimeter = 38 in
$4 + 4 + 6 + 10 + x + x + 4 = 38$ in
x = 5 in

6. 8.9 m, 7.4 m, y, 9.6 m
Perimeter = 32.6 m
$8.9 + 7.4 + 9.6 + y = 32.6$ m
y = 6.7 m

66 | Total Problems: | Total Correct: | Score: | © Carson-Dellosa CD-2215

Area of Rectangles and Parallelograms

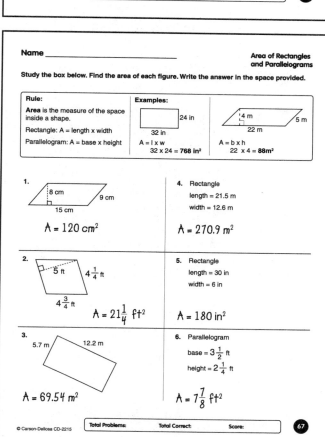

Name _____

Study the box below. Find the area of each figure. Write the answer in the space provided.

Rule:
Area is the measure of the space inside a shape.
Rectangle: A = length x width
Parallelogram: A = base x height

Examples:
24 in, 32 in
A = l x w
32 x 24 = **768 in²**

4 m, 5 m, 22 m
A = b x h
22 x 4 = **88m²**

1. 8 cm, 9 cm, 15 cm
A = 120 cm²

2. 5 ft, $4\frac{1}{4}$ ft, $4\frac{3}{4}$ ft
A = $21\frac{1}{4}$ ft²

3. 5.7 m, 12.2 m
A = 69.54 m²

4. Rectangle
length = 21.5 m
width = 12.6 m
A = 270.9 m²

5. Rectangle
length = 30 in
width = 6 in
A = 180 in²

6. Parallelogram
base = $3\frac{1}{2}$ ft
height = $2\frac{1}{4}$ ft
A = $7\frac{7}{8}$ ft²

© Carson-Dellosa CD-2215 | Total Problems: | Total Correct: | Score: | **67**

Area of Triangles and Trapezoids

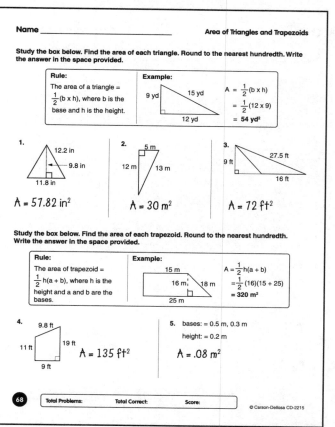

Name _____

Study the box below. Find the area of each triangle. Round to the nearest hundredth. Write the answer in the space provided.

Rule:
The area of a triangle = $\frac{1}{2}$(b x h), where b is the base and h is the height.

Example:
9 yd, 15 yd, 12 yd
$A = \frac{1}{2}$(b x h)
$= \frac{1}{2}$(12 x 9)
= 54 yd²

1. 12.2 in, 9.8 in, 11.8 in
A = 57.82 in²

2. 5 m, 12 m, 13 m
A = 30 m²

3. 9 ft, 27.5 ft, 16 ft
A = 72 ft²

Study the box below. Find the area of each trapezoid. Round to the nearest hundredth. Write the answer in the space provided.

Rule:
The area of trapezoid = $\frac{1}{2}$ h(a + b), where h is the height and a and b are the bases.

Example:
15 m, 16 m, 18 m, 25 m
$A = \frac{1}{2}$h(a + b)
$= \frac{1}{2}$ (16)(15 + 25)
= 320 m²

4. 9.8 ft, 11 ft, 19 ft, 9 ft
A = 135 ft²

5. bases: = 0.5 m, 0.3 m
height: = 0.2 m
A = .08 m²

68 | Total Problems: | Total Correct: | Score: | © Carson-Dellosa CD-2215

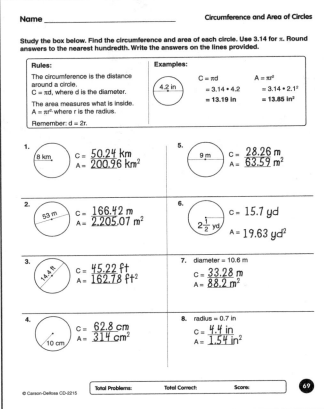

Name _____   Circumference and Area of Circles

Study the box below. Find the circumference and area of each circle. Use 3.14 for π. Round answers to the nearest hundredth. Write the answers on the lines provided.

Rules:
The circumference is the distance around a circle.
C = πd, where d is the diameter.
The area measures what is inside.
A = πr² where r is the radius.
Remember: d = 2r.

Examples:
4.2 in
C = πd
= 3.14 • 4.2
= **13.19 in**

A = πr²
= 3.14 • 2.1²
= **13.85 in²**

1. 8 km   C = 50.24 km   A = 200.96 km²
5. 9 m   C = 28.26 m   A = 63.59 m²
2. 53 m   C = 166.42 m   A = 2,205.07 m²
6. 2½ yd   C = 15.7 yd   A = 19.63 yd²
3. 14.4 ft   C = 45.22 ft   A = 162.78 ft²
7. diameter = 10.6 m   C = 33.28 m   A = 88.2 m²
4. 10 cm   C = 62.8 cm   A = 314 cm²
8. radius = 0.7 in   C = 4.4 in   A = 1.54 in²

Total Problems: Total Correct: Score: **69**

© Carson-Dellosa CD-2215

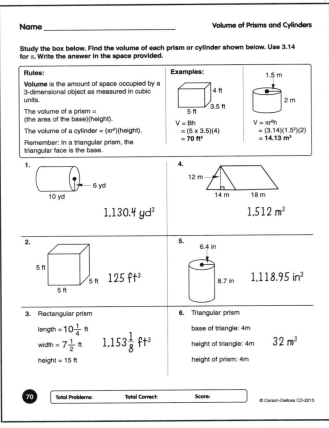

Name _____   Volume of Prisms and Cylinders

Study the box below. Find the volume of each prism or cylinder shown below. Use 3.14 for π. Write the answer in the space provided.

Rules:
Volume is the amount of space occupied by a 3-dimensional object as measured in cubic units.
The volume of a prism = (the area of the base)(height).
The volume of a cylinder = (πr²)(height).
Remember: In a triangular prism, the triangular face is the base.

Examples:
4 ft, 5 ft, 3.5 ft
V = Bh
= (5 x 3.5)(4)
= **70 ft³**

1.5 m, 2 m
V = πr²h
= (3.14)(1.5²)(2)
= **14.13 m³**

1. 6 yd, 10 yd   1,130.4 yd³
4. 12 m, 14 m, 18 m   1,512 m³
2. 5 ft, 5 ft, 5 ft   125 ft³
5. 6.4 in, 8.7 in   1,118.95 in³
3. Rectangular prism
length = 10¼ ft
width = 7½ ft
height = 15 ft   1,153⅛ ft³
6. Triangular prism
base of triangle: 4m
height of triangle: 4m
height of prism: 4m   32 m³

70   Total Problems: Total Correct: Score: © Carson-Dellosa CD-2215

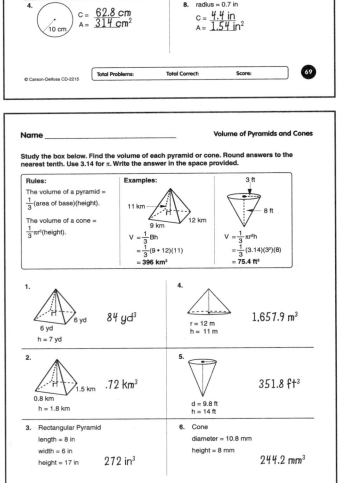

Name _____   Volume of Pyramids and Cones

Study the box below. Find the volume of each pyramid or cone. Round answers to the nearest tenth. Use 3.14 for π. Write the answer in the space provided.

Rules:
The volume of a pyramid = ⅓(area of base)(height).
The volume of a cone = ⅓πr²(height).

Examples:
11 km, 9 km, 12 km
V = ⅓Bh
= ⅓(9 • 12)(11)
= **396 km³**

3 ft, 8 ft
V = ⅓πr²h
= ⅓(3.14)(3²)(8)
= **75.4 ft³**

1. 6 yd, 6 yd, h = 7 yd   84 yd³
4. r = 12 m, h = 11 m   1,657.9 m³
2. 1.5 km, 0.8 km, h = 1.8 km   .72 km³
5. d = 9.8 ft, h = 14 ft   351.8 ft³
3. Rectangular Pyramid
length = 8 in
width = 6 in
height = 17 in   272 in³
6. Cone
diameter = 10.8 mm
height = 8 mm   244.2 mm³

Total Problems: Total Correct: Score: **71**

© Carson-Dellosa CD-2215

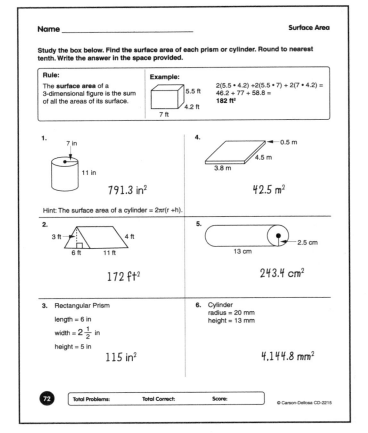

Name _____   Surface Area

Study the box below. Find the surface area of each prism or cylinder. Round to nearest tenth. Write the answer in the space provided.

Rule:
The **surface area** of a 3-dimensional figure is the sum of all the areas of its surface.

Example:
5.5 ft, 4.2 ft, 7 ft
2(5.5 • 4.2) +2(5.5 • 7) + 2(7 • 4.2) =
46.2 + 77 + 58.8 =
182 ft²

1. 7 in, 11 in   791.3 in²
4. 0.5 m, 4.5 m, 3.8 m   42.5 m²

Hint: The surface area of a cylinder = 2πr(r +h).

2. 3 ft, 4 ft, 6 ft, 11 ft   172 ft²
5. 13 cm, 2.5 cm   243.4 cm²
3. Rectangular Prism
length = 6 in
width = 2½ in
height = 5 in   115 in²
6. Cylinder
radius = 20 mm
height = 13 mm   4,144.8 mm²

72   Total Problems: Total Correct: Score: © Carson-Dellosa CD-2215